Ⓔ NGLAND

Saxon England

The Roman settlers withdrew from Britain in the 5th century, under pressure from the invading Saxons, Angles, and Jutes from Germany who drove the native Britons back into Wales, Scotland and Cornwall. It was at this time that the legendary King Arthur fought the invaders but although such a man probably existed, he almost certainly was not a king. The adventures attributed to him were more likely to have been undertaken by various warriors of the time, not by one man alone. Under the Anglo-Saxons, England was divided into seven discordant kingdoms known as the Heptarchy, made up of Wessex, Essex, Mercia, East Anglia, Kent, Sussex and Northumbria.

St Augustine was sent to England in 596 by Pope Gregory I, and Christianity subsequently spread slowly throughout those different regions. During the 7th and 8th centuries, the most powerful kingdoms were undoubtedly Wessex and Mercia but the rivalry between the different kings led to some protracted and fierce confrontations.

In 757 Offa became King of Mercia and succeeded in bringing most of England under his control. He was regarded as a great ruler but his self-regard and brutality did not earn him the love of his subjects. He was a contemporary of the Emperor Charlemagne and agreed useful trading terms with him as well as attempting to arrange a marriage between their children. Little is recorded of this period but it is clear that Offa was an effective military tactician. He established a good relationship with the pope who certainly regarded him as King of England. His enduring legacy is Offa's Dyke, an earthwork that stretches the length of the Welsh border, though whether it was built as a positive defence against the Welsh or merely as a boundary is unclear.

The struggle for supremacy between the rival kings did not abate. Egbert was declared King of Wessex in 802. He had spent time at the court of Charlemagne, possibly even joining his campaigns, so he would have learned the skills of kingship. The region grew in prosperity and power until he defeated the Mercians at the Battle of Ellandon in 825. He went on to conquer all England south of the Humber and successfully fought off the Viking invaders in the north.

It was Egbert's grandson Alfred the Great (r. 871–99) who was to make the greatest mark on history in this period. He inherited the throne from his brother Ethelred, having already demonstrated his leadership qualities in his role as second-in-command. A religious man, he also believed in military power and led his troops against three Viking invasions. In 876, the Danish leader Guthrum led a Viking invasion force into Wessex. Initially, Alfred and his men were forced to flee. (It's alleged that at some time during the next two years of hostilities, Alfred burnt the cakes his host's wife had expected him to watch and that he disguised himself as a harp player so he could infiltrate the enemy camp.) Gathering his forces, Alfred secured a resounding victory at Ethandun and subsequently agreed the Treaty of Wedmore which divided England in two, giving the Vikings 'Danelaw' (the northern part) for five years with the proviso that he would remain its overlord. This bought him time to consolidate his power and be ready for any new attack.

The Vikings, however, staged another invasion in 892 which led to four more years of fighting before finally fizzling out in the face of Alfred's superior strength. Among his key achievements were the consolidation of his kingdom, the strengthening of its defences, the building up of his army and the founding of a navy. He encouraged education in all fields, revised the legal system and began to compile the *Anglo-Saxon Chronicle* which outlined the history of the era and was kept up until the 12th century.

After Alfred's death his son Edward the Elder (r. 899–924), king of the West Saxons, continued the struggle against the Danes. He spent most of his reign fighting them for the land south of the Humber and was finally acknowledged as king of Mercia in 919. His eldest son Athelstan (r. 924–39) was to conquer the rest of the north of England, securing a final victory at Brunanburgh in 937. On coins he had himself styled *rex totius Britanniae.* Having conquered England he brokered better relations abroad by marrying off his half-sisters to various European rulers.

Athelstan's sons and successors, Edmund the Magnificent (r. 939–46), Edred (r. 946–55) and Edwy (r. 955–59), maintained the status quo. The reign of Edgar the Peaceful (r. 959–75) saw the reorganisation of the shires, defences prepared for towns, a reassessment of taxation and the start of a defined legal system. At the same time there was a flowering of learning with the production of many beautifully illustrated manuscripts. The king's chief adviser, Dunstan, Archbishop of Canterbury, embarked on a programme of monastic and Church reform. He also planned the coronation where Edgar was formally named King of England – the first time the phrase had been officially used at a coronation. The ceremony became a template for all that followed.

Ethelred the Unready

The stability of the country was short-lived. Edward the Martyr (r. 975–78) was murdered and the subsequent accession of Ethelred the Unready (r. 979–1013; 1014–16) did little for the country. Weak, indecisive and a creature of whim, Ethelred refused to heed good counsel in his policy towards the Danes, with catastrophic results. When the Danish and Norwegian kings joined forces for invasion, Ethelred bought them off by paying *danegeld*, which was essentially protection money. The army was in disarray and the prosperity of the country was disappearing fast. Suspecting a plot against his life, the king ordered the murder of all Danes in the south of England. The Danish king, Sweyn Forkbeard, took bloody revenge, forcing Ethelred to seek refuge with his brother-in-law, the Duke of Normandy. Finally, Ethelred expensively bought his way back into a brief, highly unsettled stint of power, overseeing more devastation as the country struggled against further attacks.

After Ethelred's death a battle was fought for the

English crown between his son, Edmund, and Canute, the son of Sweyn Forkbeard. A truce was reached but Edmund's sudden death meant that Canute (r. 1016–35) succeeded to the throne. In 1018 Canute was also named King of Denmark, later expanding his territories still further in 1028 when he conquered Norway. He was a strong, brave and fair leader, still famous for putting his throne in the sea to demonstrate to sycophantic courtiers that he could not command the waves to turn. He disbanded the Danish army and trusted to the loyalty of his English subjects and their desire for the much-needed stability he intended to bring. He modernised the legal system and gave generously to the Church.

Abroad, the little duchy of Normandy was quietly becoming a military force to be reckoned with. Ethelred had married Emma, daughter of Robert of Normandy, in an attempt to forge a bond with this fast-developing power. Canute did the same and married her in 1017, thereby strengthening his claim to the throne. Canute's two sons succeeded him. Harold I Harefoot (r. 1035–40) was brutish and ineffectual, while Hardicanute (r. 1040–42) was vindictive and unpopular.

When Edward the Confessor (r. 1042–66) took the crown, the country's fortunes began to turn again. He was the youngest son of Ethelred the Unready and Emma (later, wife of Canute) and had been brought up in Normandy from the age of ten. His path to the throne was smoothed by Godwinson, the powerful Earl of Wessex appointed by Canute, who saw Edward's accession as a means to strengthen his own power. Despite having taken a vow of celibacy, within a year of his coronation Edward married Emma, Godwinson's daughter. His true allegiance, though, was to the Church, one of the main achievements of his reign being the construction of Westminster Abbey.

Edward's sympathies lay with Normandy and, as his confidence grew, he appointed Normans to key political and ecclesiastical positions, thus angering Godwinson who claimed vociferously that Saxons and

Danes had the right to these posts. Edward eventually banished Godwinson and his family, but this was not a popular move. When they returned to challenge him, he was forced to reinstate them, making them even more powerful than before. Godwinson's son Harold became Edward's chief adviser and while the king devoted himself to ecclesiastical affairs, Harold became increasingly powerful, leading the army against the Welsh and believing himself to be Edward's heir apparent.

When Edward died in 1066, he left no direct heirs and the monarchy in a badly weakened state. The nobles immediately elected Harold (r. 1066) to the throne but his reign was short. William of Normandy claimed that Edward had promised *him* the English throne on a visit in 1051. Meanwhile, Harold's exiled brother Tostig had joined forces with the Norwegian king Harald Hardrada. Together they invaded Northumbria and made their way south until Harold's army stopped them at Stamford Bridge. His troops were successful but exhausted. The news that William of Normandy had landed at Pevensey and was preparing for battle could not have come at a worse moment. They marched south to confront him at Hastings where the Saxons capitulated after Harold was killed in action.

The Normans, 1066–1154

 William I (r. 1066–87)

> **Born** 1028
> **Died** 1087
> **Married** 1053, Matilda (daughter of Baldwin V of Flanders). Ten children.

Known as William the Bastard, William I was the illegitimate son of Robert I of Normandy and a second cousin of Edward the Confessor. Now recognised as William the Conqueror, his rule was characterised by harshness. Any localised Saxon rebellions were mercilessly quashed and castles built to accommodate Norman lords who then oversaw and controlled the regions. By handing the rebels' estates over to his Norman barons, William effectively wiped out the English aristocracy.

He dealt with the Church in a similar way. First, in 1070, he replaced the Archbishop of Canterbury with a

Frenchman, Lanfranc Lebec. Four other bishops were also dismissed and replaced by Europeans. From then on, whenever a bishop or abbot died, William appointed a foreign successor so that, before long, no significant religious establishment remained in English hands.

In 1086, William ordered a survey of all the English shires to discover how the wealth of his barons was being distributed. The results were recorded in the two volumes of the Domesday Book, one concerning Essex, Suffolk and Norfolk and the other the rest of England.

The following year, William was forced to return to France to continue his battles with the king who for some years had been concerned by William's increasing power. When the garrison at Mantes threatened the Norman border, William besieged the town. During the fight he sustained an injury from the pommel of his saddle which became infected. William died and was buried at St Stephen's church in Caen. As his overweight body was forced into the tomb, it burst and released a putrid smell which enveloped the congregation.

William married Matilda, daughter of Count Baldwin of Flanders, in 1053. They had ten children, four boys and six girls. The eldest, Robert, eventually rebelled against his father and sided with the King of France against him, even directly wounding him in battle. His second son, Richard, died while hunting in the New Forest. The younger sons, William and then Henry, both succeeded him as king.

 ## William II (r. 1087–1100)

Born c.1057
Died 1100

William was the third and favourite son of William the Conqueror. He had fair hair but it was his ruddy complexion that earned him the name 'Rufus'. Because of his preferred place in his father's affections, he inherited the kingdom of England whereas his oldest brother, Robert, had to be satisfied with the duchy of Normandy. William had always supported his father against his brother's open rebellion. This meant it was extremely difficult for the Norman barons who held land in both England and France to know whom to support. Matters were eventually brought to a head in 1088 by William's uncle, Odo of Bayeux, who led an uprising against him. William swiftly quelled it by devastating Odo's Kent estates. The hostility between the brothers continued well after WIlliam I's death until, in 1091, they united against the youngest brother, Henry, who boldly attempted to take control of Normandy. On the strength of that unity, William managed to persuade Robert to bring troops to England to battle successfully against Malcolm III of Scotland. Any residual enmity was quelled in 1096 when Robert pawned the duchy of Normandy to William for 10,000 marks, raising enough to support an army to accompany him on the first crusade.

William was very much his father's son – tough and uncompromising – and tried to expand his territory by frequent skirmishes with the Scots and Welsh. Malcolm

III of Scotland attempted to repossess Lothian and Northumbria but was firmly rebuffed by William who renewed the Peace of Abernethy, originally established by his father. In 1092, William commandeered some land around Carlisle. Malcolm came to negotiate but William refused to see him. On his return to Scotland, Malcolm was assassinated by Normans. William then successfully supported Malcolm's sons, Donald II and Edgar, against their uncle Donald Bane who had immediately claimed the throne of Scotland. William's smart political manoeuvring meant that his responsibility for the brothers' rule was rewarded by their subservience to him. William also wanted to gain a stronger foothold in Wales but his first attempt in 1094 failed. Four years later he tried again and gained some ground, establishing a number of castles in the Welsh Marches.

William's popularity as a leader of men was more than matched by his unpopularity with the clergy. They roundly condemned his court, which was renowned for its licentiousness. The king was rumoured to be homosexual; certainly, he never married although there was an unsubstantiated rumour that he had fathered an illegitimate son.

The Church, though, had a more serious axe to grind: William raised taxes and delayed appointing bishops or abbots so that he could collect the revenues himself. When Lanfranc, Archbishop of Canterbury, died in 1089, it took William three years to appoint a successor while he raked in the Church's money. Eventually he appointed Anselm, a Benedictine monk and scholar. Their relationship was constantly uneasy, due largely to the fact that William refused to acknowledge Urban II as the rightful pope. He called a secular court to attempt to settle their differences but Anselm appealed to Urban II, claiming religious matters could not be settled in a secular court. Eventually William agreed to acknowledge Urban II if he in turn would agree to depose Anselm. This never happened, so William continued to harass Anselm until he drove him into self-imposed exile and took over his properties.

William eventually met his death out hunting in the New Forest when he was shot by an arrow. It has never been established whether it was an accident or a conspiracy. His body was taken by peasants to Winchester where he was interred.

Henry I (r. 1100–35)

Born 1068
Died 1135
Married
(i) 1100, Mathilda (née Edith, daughter of Malcolm III of Scotland). Four children.
(ii) 1121, Adelaide (daughter of Geoffrey VII, Count of Louvain).

Although Henry, fourth son of William I, did not inherit any land from his father, he did receive a substantial sum of money and a good education. He remained discontented with his lot, though, constantly changing sides as his brothers Robert of Normandy and William II fought each other. Eventually, in 1091 he attempted a coup against them both, succeeding only in uniting his brothers against him to the extent that they agreed that, if one of them died without leaving an heir, the other would inherit. Henry was not so easily deterred. When William was killed, Robert was returning from a crusade, so Henry seized the Treasury at Winchester and rode to London where he was crowned in August 1100. The first thing he did was to decry his brother's rule and to promise good government.

Robert was having none of it. In 1101 he invaded England and negotiated an agreement whereby Henry paid him an annual sum of 3,000 marks in exchange for the kingship of England until his death. An uneasy peace was kept until 1106. At the Battle of Tinchebrai, Henry captured Robert and held him prisoner in Cardiff castle for the rest of his life. Over the next fifteen years, he secured his position in Europe by making advantageous marriages for his children.

Henry recalled Anselm, Archbishop of Canterbury, from exile. They immediately fell out because Anselm subscribed to a papal decree of 1059 which stated the papacy, not the king, should appoint the clergy. Henry would not accept this so, in 1103, Anselm went into exile again, prompting the pope to threaten Henry with excommunication. Eventually Henry agreed to accept the decree, with the proviso that he should maintain authority over the land belonging to the Church. That way he kept the revenues and had control over whoever owned the property.

Henry's most extraordinary achievement was to keep the peace in England for thirty years. During that time he established the Crown Exchequer to ensure the payment of the heavy taxes he levied to support his army abroad. He was a ruthless man, admired and feared, reputed to have pushed a man to his death from the top of Rouen castle as punishment for his disloyalty.

Henry's world crumbled when his two oldest sons drowned in the White Ship disaster off Barfleur. Despite having fathered twenty-nine children, only four were legitimate and these were his only two sons. He made his reluctant barons swear to support his oldest daughter

Matilda in the event of his death. They were further angered when Henry married her to the young Geoffrey d'Anjou in order to secure an alliance with the Angevins. When Geoffrey demanded some castles along the French coast, Henry's refusal resulted in war, Mathilda having returned to England. Henry sailed to Normandy where he fell ill with ptomaine poisoning and died.

 Stephen (r. 1135–41 [deposed]; 1141–54)

Born c.1097
Died 1154
Married c.1125, Matilda (daughter of Eustace III, Count of Boulogne). Five children.

Stephen was the nephew of Henry I. His mother, Adela, was the formidable daughter of William the Conqueror. After her husband was killed on crusade, Henry I looked after Stephen by giving him substantial lands in both France and England. Despite having sworn his allegiance to Matilda (Henry I's daughter) with the other barons at

Henry's behest, Stephen crossed the Channel and came to London immediately he heard of the king's death. He was crowned within three weeks.

He was a popular king but his reign was marked by constant civil unrest. David I of Scotland invaded Northumbria in support of Matilda but he was defeated by Stephen at the Battle of the Standard in 1138. The same year, Stephen confiscated Robert of Gloucester's properties in the Welsh Marches while Robert, an illegitimate son of Henry I, was in Normandy. As Stephen's support began to dwindle, he made a number of crucial errors that seriously damaged his position: he alienated his brother Henry by refusing to support his claim to the archbishopric of Canterbury; he arrested three influential bishops, thus laying himself open to the charge of violating Church authority; and he gave Carlisle castle to the Scots.

In 1139 Robert and Matilda landed their troops on the south coast of England and the first English civil war began. They finally defeated Stephen at Lincoln in 1141 and imprisoned him in Bristol castle. Matilda declared herself queen while retaining the title 'Empress'. Her term was brief and when Bishop Henry rejoined his brother's cause, the tide of opinion turned and she was forced to flee London before her coronation could take place. Her final misfortune was the capture of Robert by Stephen's supporters at Wherwell. Matilda had no choice but to agree to an exchange of prisoners – Robert for Stephen. Stephen was crowned for a second time on Christmas Day 1141.

The civil war continued until Robert of Gloucester's death in 1147 whereupon Matilda left England for good. By this time Stephen was hardly fit to rule the country, constantly thwarted by the Archbishop of Canterbury who refused to approve the planned succession of Stephen's son, Eustace. Meanwhile, trouble was brewing in Normandy where Matilda's husband Geoffrey d'Anjou had taken advantage of the war in England and was virtually in control. In 1153, their son Henry Fitzempress sailed to England to assert his claim to the throne. He was successfully rebuffed until Eustace died of a seizure, aged twenty-two. Stephen gave in and signed the Treaty of Wallingford in which he acknowledged Henry as his rightful heir.

Stephen spent his last year in Kent, suffering from piles and finally dying of appendicitis. He was buried alongside his beloved wife and son in Faversham Abbey.

The Plantagenets, 1154–1399

 Henry II (r. 1154–89)

Born 1133
Died 1189
Married 1152, Eleanor of Aquitaine (daugher of William X of Aquitaine). Eight children.

When Henry II took the crown of England in 1154, his empire stretched from the Scottish border down to the Pyrenees. His inheritance of Normandy, Maine, Touraine and Anjou at his father's death in 1151 was augmented by his marriage to Eleanor of Aquitaine, former wife of Louis VII of France, in 1152.

In 1162 Thomas à Becket was elected Archbishop of Canterbury. The two men had been friends for years and Henry thought Becket would help him reform the Church. However, in demonstrating his loyalty to the Church in the face of his critics, Becket proved an unpredictable ally. Matters came to a head in 1164 when

Henry introduced the Constitutions of Clarendon. They proposed that if any member of the clergy were charged with a criminal offence, his trial could be held in a civil court with no recourse of appeal to the pope without the king's consent. Initially Becket agreed, but then changed his mind. Henry was furious and charged him with various offences. He was found guilty, forced to forfeit his estates and fled into exile in France. In 1170, he returned to England, roundly condemning anyone involved with the coronation of Henry's son, Henry, the 'Young King'. (It was common practice in France to secure the succession before the reigning king died; this was the only time it happened in England.) Frustrated by his behaviour, Henry notoriously cried out: 'Is there none will rid me of this turbulent priest?' He was overheard by four knights who took him at his word and rode to Canterbury where they murdered Becket in the cathedral. Henry was horrified, wore sackcloth and apologised to the pope. Becket was canonised in 1173.

Henry worked hard to keep his empire intact. He

was tireless in his efforts to restore peace and justice to his domains, introducing legal reforms, re-establishing the jury system and reducing the power of the barons. In 1155 a papal bull gave him authority over all of Britain so he was able to restore order by destroying many of the castles built during the civil war, negotiating for Northumbria and Cumbria with the Scots and subduing the Welsh. In 1171 he invaded Ireland, quickly establishing authority over Leinster and Meath. The Irish bishops agreed to various reforms to bring the Church of Ireland in line with the Catholic Church. In 1177, Henry's youngest son John was honoured with the title Lord of Ireland, though it meant little.

Henry made some sound dynastic marriages for his children, initially securing himself as one of the most powerful men in Europe. However, it was his family that was to cause him most grief in his last years. His marriage with Eleanor had not been happy. She encouraged their sons to rebel against him. The 'Young King' died of a fever in 1183 and their third son Geoffrey died in an accident three years later. When Henry discovered that his favourite son, John, was siding with his brother Richard and Philippe II of France, he was broken-hearted and submitted to them in 1189. He died two days later in Chinon. Eleanor outlived him by an astonishing fifteen years, dying at the age of eighty-two.

 Richard I (r. 1189–99)

Born 1157
Died 1199
Married 1191, Berengaria (daughter of Sancho VI, King of Navarre). No children.

Though his fame is as the hero Richard the Lionheart, Richard I spent only six months in England during his ten-year reign and had little interest in the financial or administrative government of his kingdom. Brought up in Aquitaine, he learned the skills of soldiering which he honed in his attacks on his father, Henry II. He inherited the title of Duke of Aquitaine from his mother Eleanor.

Richard I

When Henry II died, Richard inherited the title of Duke of Normandy then rode to London to be crowned in 1189. His coronation was marred by a massacre of Jews in London, shortly to be followed by others in cities further north. Richard stayed in England long enough to raise money to finance his part in the crusades. He did this by selling lands that belonged to both state and Church, selling charters of self-government to towns and, most notably, selling Scotland to William the Lyon for 10,000 marks.

Richard then joined forces with Philippe II of France and rode with him to the Holy Land in 1190, leaving England in the capable hands of the chancellor, William of Longchamp. Richard angered Philippe en route by refusing to marry his daughter, despite their twenty-year betrothal. Philippe rode ahead leaving Richard to conquer Cyprus after the ship carrying his sister Joan and his new bride Berengaria was almost captured. He married Berengaria in Limassol before continuing east. Having successfully concluded the siege of Acre, he marched south, defeating Saladin at Arsouf, then sailed for home. However, his ship was wrecked and he was forced to travel by land. He was captured by Prince Leopold of Austria who passed him to Henry II of Germany who held him hostage for fifteen months. Legend has it that the minstrel Blondel travelled Austria until he tracked him down and negotiated the ransom.

Meanwhile, back home, Richard's brother John was threatening to usurp the throne. By the time Richard returned in 1194, the Treasury was drained and territories lost in France. Richard forgave his brother but spent the rest of his rule reconquering his French lands. Finally, during the siege of Chalus in 1199, he was shot by an arrow. The wound turned gangrenous and he died a few days later.

John (r. 1199–1216)

Born 1167
Died 1216
Married
(i) 1189, Isabella (daughter of William, Earl of Gloucester). No children. Divorced 1199.
(ii) 1200, Isabella (daughter of Count of Angoulême). Five children.

John was the youngest of Henry II and Eleanor of Aquitaine's children, also known as Lackland because he did not inherit any property. In 1177 Henry II did give him the nominal title of Lord of Ireland but it came without authority or land. Richard the Lionheart named him as his successor and John was crowned in 1199. The same year he divorced his first wife and married Isabella of Angoulême. Not surprisingly, her fiancé objected and took his complaint to Philippe II who immediately confiscated John's lands in France. John reacted quickly in defence of his territory, but made the mistake of capturing his own nephew, Arthur of Brittany, who was favoured by many as a future king. Arthur was never seen again. John was forced to return to England, having lost almost everything.

John also infuriated the pope by refusing to accept John Langton as Archbishop of Canterbury. In 1208, Innocent III suspended all Church services in England and excommunicated the king. Not that John was particularly worried, since it now meant he could put the Church's revenues towards the military campaign he planned against France and into his various skirmishes with the English barons, many of whom were about to be ruined by his policy of high taxation. In 1212, rumours of a baronial plot and a planned invasion by Philippe II made John realise that the isolation imposed by his excommunication put him in an extremely vulnerable position. As a result, he re-established relations with the pope, making England a fief of the papacy and paying homage to the pope as his feudal lord. Innocent III could not resist.

Henry III

Strengthened by the support of the pope, John campaigned against Philippe only to lose to him at the Battle of Bouvines in 1214. The English barons rebelled in the face of this defeat and made John sign the Magna Carta at Runnymede in 1215. Within months, John had broken its terms with the support of the pope and civil war broke out again. The barons urged the French prince Louis to England to champion their cause. John was forced to retreat across the Wash towards Lincoln. However, he misjudged the tides and all his valuables, including the crown, were lost. He caught a fever which, aggravated by his gluttony, led to dysentery. Within days he was dead.

Henry III (r. 1216–72)

Born 1207
Died 1272
Married 1236, Eleanor (daughter of Count of Provence). Nine children.

Henry was only nine when he was hastily crowned in Gloucester Cathedral with his mother's bracelet for a crown, the real one having been lost in the Wash. He inherited a country in a state of civil war but his regent, William Marshal, and his justiciar, Hubert de Burgh, were effective in restoring law and order among the barons and in persuading Prince Louis to return to France. In 1220, Henry was again crowned but with due ceremony at Westminster though his direct rule did not commence until 1227. Until then Hubert de Burgh retained the role of regent that he had taken on at William Marshal's death. In 1232, de Burgh was dismissed on a trumped-up charge of treason.

Henry's foreign policy was a disaster and resulted in his losing almost all his lands in France. At home, he ignored the terms of the Magna Carta and filled his court with Europeans, particularly after his marriage to Eleanor. The barons were enraged by his behaviour, not to mention the heavy taxes being exacted from them to be squandered on unsuccessful foreign campaigns. On the other hand, Henry did encourage the development of literature, arts and architecture, the rebuilding of Westminster Abbey and the construction of Salisbury Cathedral.

From 1258, the barons' objections became more forceful as a determined leader emerged from their ranks: Simon de Montfort, Henry's brother-in-law. Henry was forced to recognise the Provisions of Oxford which limited royal power. But not for long. He obtained the support of the pope in denouncing de Montfort and the country fell into civil war once more. In 1264 de Montfort captured Henry and his son Edward at Lewes. A parliament was called to force Henry's submission. However, his son continued the fight and de Montfort was killed at the Battle of Evesham in 1265. Henry immediately overturned the acts of parliament that had been forced on him and meted out vicious retribution on any rebel barons. From then on he left much of the government to his son, succumbing to dementia made worse by his grief at the death of his brother Richard in 1272, dying himself seven months later.

 ## Edward I (r. 1272–1307)

Born 1239
Died 1307
Married
   (i) 1254, Eleanor (daughter of Ferdinand III, King of Castile). Sixteen children.
   (ii) 1299, Margaret (daughter of Philippe III of France). Three children.

Having supported his father in the civil wars, Edward left for the crusades in 1270. He heard of his father's death in 1272 when returning with his wife via Sicily but he did not arrive in London to take up his crown until 1274.

Edward immediately introduced tax and legislative reforms which went towards the eventual formation of the Model Parliament in 1295 in which each shire was represented by lords, clergy and people's representatives. In 1290 he expelled all the Jews from England on charges of usury and seized their assets.

Determined to unite England with Scotland and Wales, in 1276 Edward invaded North Wales to force Prince Llywelyn ap Gruffydd into submission. A further rebellion resulted in Llywelyn's death and in 1284 Wales finally became part of the king's dominion. After further rebellions he made his son Prince of Wales in 1301. To uphold his rule, Edward authorised the building of a number of castles in the north of the country.

Edward campaigned vigorously to assert his rule over Scotland, earning the name 'Hammer of the Scots'. After Alexander III's death in 1286, the succession to the Scottish throne was in dispute. Initially he supported the claim of the four-year-old Margaret of Norway. Her early death meant an interregnum while Edward was called upon to adjudicate between the many contenders for the throne. He chose John Balliol, a weak man who was easily incited into rebellion by the Scots. Edward took him prisoner at Berwick and claimed the kingship for himself, removing the Stone of Scone to Westminster. Over the next few years he tried to quell the rebellious Scots, capturing their leader William Wallace in 1298 at the Battle of Falkirk. A new leader, Robert the Bruce, took over immediately. Edward rode north to confront him but died of dysentery in 1307, leaving the dispute unsettled.

Edward II (r. 1307–27)

Born 1284
Died 1327
Married 1308, Isabelle (daughter of Philippe IV of France). Four children.

The youngest son of Edward I and Eleanor, Edward II had little interest in his responsibilities as King of England. Despite his father's entreaties to continue the struggle for Scotland, he made a couple of sorties across the border then left it to Robert the Bruce. It was not until 1314 that he decided to bring Scotland under his control but he was roundly beaten at the Battle of Bannockburn.

Edward fell under the influence of the Gascon prince Piers Gaveston early in his reign, showering him with favours, even leaving him as regent while he went to France for his marriage. Feelings against Gaveston ran high. In 1310 parliament authorised the Lords Ordainers, a team of barons led by Thomas, Earl of Lancaster, to take control from the king. Gaveston was exiled but on his return captured by the disaffected Earl of Warwick and beheaded. Edward soon found new favourites in Sir Hugh Despenser and his son. In 1322 he quelled a rebellion led by Lancaster at the Battle of Boroughbridge.

The biggest threat to Edward came from his estranged wife. She and her lover Sir Roger Mortimer sailed from France to depose Edward in favour of his son (Edward III), executing many of his supporters including the Despensers. Edward was imprisoned in Berkeley Castle where he was famously murdered by a red hot poker inserted in his backside.

Edward III (r. 1327–77)

Born 1312
Died 1377
Married 1328, Philippa (daughter of William V, Count of Hainault and Holland).
Thirteen children.

Edward was only fourteen when he came to the throne so Sir Roger Mortimer acted as regent. After three years, Edward had had enough and he ordered Mortimer to be taken to Tyburn where he was hung, drawn and quartered.

Unlike his father, Edward decided he needed the support of the barons so he instituted a programme of legal and administrative reforms. These included dividing parliament into two houses, and establishing English rather than French as the language to be spoken there and in the law courts. Various statutes were introduced to define treason, to establish the king's authority over ecclesiastical appointments, to give parliament control over raising taxes and to establish the office of Justice of the Peace.

Edward's reign was dominated by the Hundred Years War which began in 1337. In 1340, he declared himself King of France through his mother's line. The war raged intermittently, with Edward's fortunes continually changing, claiming major victories at the battles of Crécy and Poitiers.

In 1349 the Black Death swept through Europe and is believed to have killed half the population of England, devastating its militia. Edward's eldest son, the Black Prince, responsible for the English military successes, was forced through ill-health to hand command to his brother, John of Gaunt, who could not boast any of his fighting skills.

By 1374, all Edward had of France was Calais and a little strip of the coast. Edward died an unhappy man, leaving the country in poverty.

Richard II (r. 1377–99)

Born 1367
Died 1400
Married
   (i) 1382, Anne (daughter of Charles IV, Holy Roman Emperor). No children.
   (ii) 1396, Isabella (daughter of Charles VI of France). No children.

Son of the popular Black Prince, Richard was only ten when he came to the throne. Initially parliament ran the country but power soon devolved, principally into the hands of his uncle, John of Gaunt. Richard first showed his metal over the Peasants' Revolt in 1381, when Wat Tyler led his supporters to London to protest against the levying of a poll tax to finance wars against Ireland, France, Scotland and Wales. Richard rode out to appease the rebels, making promises he would never deliver. In the ensuing scuffle, Tyler was killed and the mob was persuaded to return home peacefully.

Richard II

Trouble also came from the barons who disliked the way Richard distributed his favours in court without consulting parliament. The opposition was led by five Lords Appellant (including Henry Bolingbroke, son of John of Gaunt) who effectively governed until Richard declared himself of age in 1389. He then took control of parliament and swiftly took brutal revenge on the Lords Appellant, exiling Bolingbroke to France. When John of Gaunt died, Richard seized his estates. Bolingbroke returned for his inheritance and succeeded in forcing Richard's abdication in 1399.

Richard was imprisoned in Pontefract castle where he is believed to have starved himself to death in 1400.

The House of Lancaster, 1399–1461

 Henry IV (r. 1399–1413)

Born 1367
Died 1413
Married
(i) 1381, Mary (daughter of Humphrey de Bohun, Earl of Hereford). Seven children.
(ii) 1402, Joan (daughter of Charles II of Navarre). No children.

Henry's rule was a troubled one, marked by continual squabbles with parliament over raising money to finance his army. Within months of being crowned, he had to put down a rebellion masterminded by Richard II's cronies whom he dealt with harshly, dismembering them and bringing them back to London in sacks. Although the French staged an invasion of the south coast, they were preoccupied throughout most of Henry's reign with their own civil war.

Henry took James I of Scotland hostage and, by keeping him at court, relations between the two countries remained calm. More troublesome were the Welsh. In 1400, Owain Glyndwr staged a revolt to obtain Welsh independence. Henry dealt with it swiftly but over the next few years Glyndwr used guerrilla warfare and enlisted the support of various disillusioned English rebels, including Henry 'Hotspur' Percy, to challenge Henry again. Once again, Henry defeated them, killing Hotspur, although the rebellion continued to simmer until his definitive victory in 1408 when the prime movers were dealt with mercilessly.

Henry's last years were overshadowed by illness, particularly a form of eczema which many mistook for leprosy. He also had to deal with his son, Henry of Monmouth, thought to be planning a coup against him after he had refused to abdicate in his favour. However, before anything happened, the king died.

Henry V (r. 1413–22)

Born 1387
Died 1422
Married 1420, Catherine (daughter of Charles VI of France). One son.

Henry's early experience fighting with his father against the Welsh stood him in good stead for reopening the Hundred Years War against France. Determined to win back lands that had once belonged to England, he secured the support of parliament and took virtually all the English nobility with him to invade France in 1415. Within a few weeks he had taken the port of Harfleur and then fought the Battle of Agincourt where he lost 400 men against 6,000 Frenchmen who died. Henry conquered Normandy in 1419, then signed the Treaty of Troyes which named him as regent of France and heir to the French throne. The pact was sealed by Henry's marriage to Charles VI's daughter Catherine in 1420. They returned victoriously to England, but in 1422 he died of dysentery, ten months after the birth of his son. Charles VI died six weeks later, leaving the baby Henry king of both England and France.

 Henry VI (r. 1422–61 [deposed]; 1470–71)

Born 1421
Died 1471
Married 1445, Margaret of Anjou (daughter of René, Duke of Anjou and King of Naples).
One son.

Not a man cut out for kingship, Henry was modest and peaceable, a profoundly religious man remembered for founding Eton and King's College, Cambridge. As he was only ten months old when he came to the throne, John, Duke of Bedford, became regent of France while Humphrey, Duke of Gloucester was appointed protector of England. Bedford did his best to maintain England's hold on France, but the French were dissatisfied with the state of affairs. They soon rallied to the call of Joan of Arc, a peasant girl who claimed to have had a vision that told her to drive the English from France. She was burned at the stake in 1431 but the French pursued her cause until, in 1453, the English had been driven out from all but Calais.

At home, the court was divided by rivalry and suspicion. The appointment of the Duke of Somerset as Henry's adviser enraged Richard, Duke of York, great-grandson of Edward III, who returned from exile in Ireland demanding a seat on the council on the strength of his position as next in line to the throne. Suddenly and unexpectedly, Henry suffered a bout of insanity, and Richard was appointed Protector of the Realm. His rivalry with Somerset led to the Wars of the Roses, the red rose symbolising the Lancastrians, and the white symbolising the Yorkists. As Henry recovered his sanity, York was released from his duties as protector and Margaret took charge, leading to their confrontation at St Albans in 1455. Margaret supported the Duke of Somerset and was active in raising armies to rout the arrogant York. In 1460 Henry was captured at Northampton and forced to recognise Richard of York as heir. Margaret rallied the troops and York was killed at Wakefield. Henry was released but by this time was clearly insane.

In 1461 Richard of York's son, Edward, defeated the Lancastrians at Towton and Margaret fled with Henry to Scotland. Edward took the throne from 1461 to 1470, when it briefly returned to Henry, and then from 1471 after the latter's defeat at Mortimer's Cross. Henry was imprisoned in the Tower of London where he was murdered.

The House of York, 1461–1485

 Edward IV (r. 1461–70; 1471–83)

Born 1442
Died 1483
Married 1464, Elizabeth Woodville (daughter of Richard Woodville, 1st Earl Rivers).
Ten children.

Tall, handsome and an incorrigible womaniser, Edward none the less brought beneficial changes to England. His cousin Richard, Earl of Warwick, known as the 'Kingmaker', was instrumental in bringing him to the throne. Warwick helped defeat the Lancastrians and played a key role in the government. However, he was infuriated by Edward's secret marriage to Elizabeth Woodville which scotched his negotiations with Louis XI of France for Edward to marry a French princess.

Eventually Warwick became so disillusioned with Edward that he changed sides, supporting Edward's brother, George, Duke of Clarence, against him. After one unsuccessful rebellion, he staged another with the support of Louis XI and Margaret of Anjou. Edward fled to France. Warwick brought Henry VI out of the Tower to restore him to the throne in 1470. A year later, Edward returned to defeat Warwick at the Battle of Barnet and ordered the murder of Henry. His crown secure, Edward determined to regain lands lost to France. He managed to rally the support of Brittany, Aragon and Burgundy but, when the time came to confront Louis XI, the French dukes let him down. The only solution was to agree to a seven-year truce. Meanwhile, back in England, the Duke of Clarence continued his plotting for the throne. Edward had had enough and in 1478 tried his brother for treason. Clarence was imprisoned in the Tower where he is said to have been drowned in a butt of Malmsey wine.

Edward's reign was otherwise marked by his attention to commercial and legislative reform, fulfilling the promises made in the original Yorkist manifestos. He was also a patron of the arts and a friend and patron of William Caxton who introduced the first printing press into England. The king's health began to fail in his late thirties and he died, perhaps from pneumonia though some have attributed his early death to over-eating.

 Edward V (r. 1483)

Born 1470
Died 1483

When Edward IV died, his sons Edward and Richard, the 'Princes in the Tower', were brought to London for Edward's coronation. In his will, Edward IV had appointed his brother Richard, Duke of Gloucester, as Lord High Protector of the Realm. Richard met the boys at Ludlow and escorted them to the Tower of London where they were to stay in the royal apartments. Days before the coronation, the princes were declared illegitimate by parliament, on the grounds that Edward IV had married Elizabeth Woodville when he was betrothed to Lady Eleanor Butler. Richard was declared king. The two princes were last seen in the Tower of London where they are believed to have been murdered by Richard. No proof has ever been found.

 Richard III (r. 1483–85)

Born 1452
Died 1485
Married 1472, Anne Neville (daughter of Richard Neville, Earl of Warwick). One child.

The last of the Plantagenets, Richard's image has been blackened over the years, not least by the belief that he ordered the murder of the Princes in the Tower to ensure his succession to the throne. Until that point he was a loyal supporter of his brother, Edward IV, particularly through his management of the north of England which he effectively ruled on Edward's behalf, becoming known as 'Lord of the North'. His marriage to the daughter of the Earl of Warwick secured him half the

Warwick estates, much to the annoyance of George, Duke of Clarence, who, unlike Richard, had supported Warwick against Edward IV and felt he had a claim to them. Richard had one son, Edward, who died in 1484 aged eight. His wife was too frail to have more children and died the following year.

Richard's reign was brief and characterised by his struggles to keep the crown. The Duke of Buckingham, previously his supporter, turned his back on the king and allied himself with Edward IV's queen, Elizabeth Woodville, and Henry Tudor, an exiled Lancastrian and descendant of Edward III. The duke's rebellion was quashed and he was summarily executed at Salisbury in 1483. Undaunted, Henry Tudor went on to forge an alliance with Charles VIII of France who supported his invasion of England in 1485. The armies clashed at the Battle of Bosworth. Richard was determined to have direct combat with Henry Tudor himself. Instead he was killed and his naked body was carried on a pack horse to Leicester where it was displayed for two days.

The Tudors, 1485–1603

 Henry VII (r. 1485–1509)

Born 1457
Died 1509
Married 1486, Elizabeth of York (daughter of
Edward IV). Eight children.

A Welshman, brought up mostly in exile in France,
Henry Tudor was keen to secure his position
immediately. Although he could pretend a tenuous claim
to the throne, he came to it by right of conquest. In 1486,
he married Elizabeth of York, daughter of Edward IV,
thus uniting the houses of York and Lancaster, putting
an end to the Wars of the Roses and strengthening his
claim to the throne. He betrothed his eldest son, Arthur,
to Catherine of Aragon, daughter of Ferdinand and
Isabella of Spain. Only weeks after their wedding in
1499 Arthur died of consumption. Henry also tried to
forge alliances with Scotland by offering the hands of his

daughters Margaret and Mary. Margaret was betrothed to James IV although Mary remained single for another fifteen years. A peace treaty was finally agreed with Scotland in 1502. Henry's policy of appointing Welsh lords to court and granting them rights to Welsh territory, especially in the Marches, meant that peace reigned there too.

The principal threat to Henry's throne came from two 'Pretenders'. The first, Lambert Simnel, claiming to be the Earl of Warwick, was championed by the Earl of Lincoln. Simnel was taken to Ireland for his own safety where, in 1487, he was crowned Edward VI. Henry declared him a fake but still had to counter an invasion led by Lincoln. Henry's troops were victorious at the Battle of Stoke. Simnel was pardoned and put to work in the royal kitchens. The second was Perkin Warbeck who claimed to be Richard, the youngest of the Princes in the Tower. He gathered the support of the King of France, Margaret of Burgundy and Emperor Maximilian, not to mention various English barons. Henry executed the barons so that when Warbeck arrived from France he found little support. He went to Scotland and with the support of James IV tried to challenge Henry again. His campaign was a failure. The only place left for him to go was Cornwall which had rebelled against paying the high taxes recently levied by Henry. Warbeck was defeated again and put in the Tower, to be executed for treason in 1499.

During his reign, Henry was anxious to reduce the power of the barons, which he effectively did by taxing them heavily. He also banned their private armies and re-established the Court of Star Chamber which could try any nobleman who broke the law. Henry was interested in trade and exploration, helping to finance the Cabot brothers' voyages to America. He encouraged building, incorporating the Henry VII chapel into Westminster Abbey, building Richmond Palace and rebuilding Greenwich Palace. When he died, he left a united country and a full Treasury.

Henry VIII (r. 1509–47)

Born 1491
Died 1547
Married

(i) 1509, Catherine of Aragon (daughter of Ferdinand II of Aragon). Six children. Annulled 1533.

(ii) 1533, Anne Boleyn (daughter of Thomas Boleyn, Earl of Wiltshire). Three children. Beheaded 1536.

(iii) 1536, Jane Seymour (daughter of Sir John Seymour). One child. Died 1536.

(iv) 1540, Anne of Cleves (daughter of Johann, Duke of Cleves). No children. Annulled 1540.

(v) 1540, Catherine Howard (daughter of Lord Edmund Howard). No children. Beheaded.

(vi) 1543, Catherine Parr (daughter of Sir Thomas Parr). No children.

Henry VIII

Henry was the larger-than-life third son of Henry VII. On his accession to the throne he obeyed his father's wish and married his brother Arthur's widow, Catherine of Aragon. He was a well-educated man, skilled at languages, dancing, music and hunting. His first interest was to establish himself in Europe and so he joined the Holy League, formed by Pope Julius II, Venice and Spain against France. Scotland's King James IV objected strongly to this alliance and took advantage of Henry being in France to invade England, only to fall at the Battle of Flodden in 1513. His heir, James V, was only one year old so his mother Margaret, Henry's sister, became regent and peace between the countries was restored.

While busy with affairs abroad, Henry appointed Thomas Wolsey to the post of Lord Chancellor, relying on him to run the country. In Europe, the anti-Catholic ideas of German theologian Martin Luther were encouraging the growth of Protestantism. Henry wrote *The Defence of the Seven Sacraments* in support of the pope who rewarded him with the title Defender of the Faith.

Father to one surviving daughter (Mary) and anxious for a male heir, Henry persuaded Wolsey to petition Rome for an annulment of his first marriage. Wolsey's failure led to his arrest for treason in 1529. Thomas Cromwell, now Henry's adviser, persuaded him to break with the Church of Rome and to establish a separate Church of England with himself at its head. Thomas Cranmer, Archbishop of Canterbury, duly declared the marriage annulled and blessed the wedding to Anne Boleyn. Henry was excommunicated in 1533 and the following year the Act of Supremacy established Henry as head of the Church of England. Henry ordered a commission under Thomas Cromwell to investigate the affairs of the monasteries. The dissolution of the smaller ones in 1536 and of all the others in 1539 provided the king with much-needed finance. Any resistance was swiftly dealt with. Funds were used, among other things, to increase the size of the navy, to found Trinity College, Cambridge, to build St James's Palace and to enlarge Hampton Court. In 1536 Henry achieved the Act of Union between Wales and England. Unable to effect the same arrangement with Ireland, he declared himself King of Ireland in 1542.

Since Henry had tired of Anne Boleyn and her only surviving child (Elizabeth) was a daughter, he readily accepted invented charges of her infidelity. Archbishop Cranmer announced the marriage null and void a couple of days before Henry ordered her execution in 1536. Henry then married Jane Seymour who gave him his longed-for son but died in the process. Cromwell negotiated Henry's next marriage to Anne of Cleves. Henry, however, was disappointed because her appearance did not live up to her portrait and, fearing a political backlash if he reneged on the deal, ensured that the marriage remained unconsummated and had it declared null and void too. Cromwell was arrested and executed on charges of treason in the same year.

Henry's fifth wife, Catherine Howard, was thirty years younger than he was. Within months she had taken lovers more her own age. Initially resistant to the accusations, Henry eventually charged her with treason and she was executed. By this time, Henry was more in need of a carer than a wife, so in 1543 he settled on the twice-widowed Catherine Parr who also proved to be a good step-mother. After his death in 1547, aged fifty-five, he was buried alongside Jane Seymour in St George's Chapel, Windsor.

Edward VI (r. 1547–53)

Born 1537
Died 1553

The son of Henry VIII and Jane Seymour, Edward was a precocious and sickly nine-year-old when he acceded to the throne. His uncle Edward Seymour, Earl of Hertford, was made Duke of Somerset and Protector of the Realm. Seymour immediately invaded Scotland in an attempt to forge a marriage between Edward and Mary, Queen of Scots, a union originally proposed by Henry VIII. Despite his 1547 victory at the Battle of Pinkie, he was unable to bring this about. Edward was forced to agree to the execution of his uncle for treason and blamed his other uncle, Edward Seymour, who was in turn executed in 1552. The new protector was John Dudley, Earl of Warwick and Duke of Northumberland.

The Reformation begun under Henry VIII was consolidated with the 1549 First Act of Uniformity, which declared the Catholic mass illegal, and the introduction of a new Book of Common Prayer. Edward also gave his name to numerous schools throughout the country and established the poorhouse of Bridewell and Christ's Hospital. He died from tuberculosis and syphilis aged fifteen.

Jane (r. 1553)

> **Born** 1537
> **Died** 1554
> **Married** 1553, Guilford (son of John Dudley, Duke of Northumberland).
> No children.

Lady Jane Grey, the granddaughter of Henry VIII's sister Mary, was named by Edward VI as his successor. Northumberland, the protector, orchestrated her marriage to his son shortly before she acceded to the throne. A staunch Protestant, she was thought to be a safeguard against the Catholicism represented by Mary. There was a public outcry, Northumberland's army was defeated and he was executed. Jane (the 'Nine-days Queen') and her husband were imprisoned in the Tower. She was executed in 1554.

 Mary I (r. 1553–58)

> **Born** 1516
> **Died** 1558
> **Married** 1554, Philip (son of Charles V, Holy Roman Emperor). No children.

Mary was the only surviving child from Henry VIII's marriage to Catherine of Aragon. Like her mother she was a devout Catholic and refused to recognise her father as head of the Church. When she was older, she continued to celebrate the Catholic mass. Mary's childhood was a miserable one thanks to the long-drawn-out divorce between her parents. She was pronounced illegitimate in 1533 and was sent away from her mother to be brought up with her half-sister Elizabeth.

On Edward VI's death, she was the popular choice for queen. She rode with Elizabeth from Framlingham to London to claim the throne. One of her first concerns was to persuade parliament to unpick the Protestant reforms, among other things reinstating the Latin mass and her own legitimacy. In 1554 the papal legate announced that England was restored to the Papal See and Mary's reign of terror began. Heretics were burned at the stake, including Thomas Cranmer and other members of the clergy who refused to abandon their Protestant beliefs.

Her other preoccupation was finding a husband and producing a Catholic heir. She fixed on Philip of Spain, son of the Holy Roman Emperor, but her choice was unpopular with many who considered it a potential threat to England's independence. Sir Thomas Wyatt incited revolt, but the uprising was crushed and he was executed. Mary believed her half-sister Elizabeth was involved and had her imprisoned briefly in the Tower before confining her to Woodstock and then Hatfield. The royal couple were married, but whereas Mary loved her husband, he considered it a marriage of political convenience and soon returned to Spain, returning briefly only once, in 1557. That year England and Spain declared war against France which resulted in the loss of Calais, the one bit of France that England had held on to since the end of the Hundred Years War. Mary was devastated and famously remarked that when she was dead, 'you will find Philip and Calais engraved on my heart'. She died the following year and was buried at Westminster Abbey.

Elizabeth I

Elizabeth I (r. 1558–1603)

Born 1533
Died 1603

Elizabeth was the only daughter of Henry VIII and Anne Boleyn and the only child of Henry's not to have contracted his syphilis. She was declared illegitimate after her mother's execution but Henry was eventually forced to reinstate her in the order of succession. When she inherited the throne on the death of her half-sister, Mary, she also inherited a country divided by religion. One of her first duties was to resolve the problem and she decided to take a middle path between the two extremes. Protestantism was adopted as the national religion and the 1559 Act of Supremacy named her Supreme Governor of the Church of England. However, the services remained similar to the old Catholic services and Catholic mass could be heard in private. The pope reacted by excommunicating her, but Elizabeth was undeterred.

Elizabeth never married, revelling in her status as the

'Virgin Queen' whose only partner was England. However, she was not short of suitors from both home and abroad. Her favourite was Robert Dudley, Earl of Leicester, but he was rumoured to have killed his wife, making him an unsuitable match. Elizabeth refused to give in to her age, donning a red wig and whitening her face to hide the smallpox scars. She loved jewels and owned many elaborate costumes.

Relations with Scotland were strained thanks to the claim to the English throne made by Mary, Queen of Scots, Elizabeth's cousin and wife of the King of France, François II. After his sudden death in 1560, there were fears that Mary would marry a powerful heir to a European throne and that together they might invade England and topple Elizabeth. Instead, she married Lord Darnley and had one son before Darnley died in mysterious circumstances. That, the murder of her secretary Rizzio and her rapid marriage to Lord Bothwell destroyed her credibility and she was driven from Scotland to beg for Elizabeth's help. As a possible

Elizabeth I

Catholic figurehead, she presented a real threat. Elizabeth felt she had no alternative but to keep her prisoner for eighteen years. When, in 1586, Mary was implicated in the Babington plot against the queen's life, Elizabeth was forced to execute her.

Early on in her reign, Elizabeth supported the Protestant Huguenots in the religious wars in France but subsequently things were relatively quiet until, in 1587, Sir Francis Drake attacked the Spanish fleet in Cadiz harbour. In 1588, Philip II of Spain launched the Spanish Armada against the English Navy but was defeated.

By the end of her reign, England was experiencing a 'golden age', with London prospering and England home to a flowering of the arts with writers such as Shakespeare, Spenser, Marlowe, and Jonson and composers such as William Byrd. Trade had expanded and the Treasury was strong. When Elizabeth died, she was buried alongside Mary I in Westminster Abbey. Although she left no formal will, she had agreed that James VI of Scotland should be her successor.

The Stuarts, 1603–1714

 James I (r. 1603–25); also James VI of Scotland

Born 1566
Died 1625
Married 1589, Anne (daughter of Frederick II of Denmark and Oslo). Nine children.

Nicknamed the 'wisest fool in christendom', James had already been King of Scotland for thirty-six years when he inherited the English throne from Elizabeth. The war between England and Spain still raged but, because of Scotland's historical friendship with Spain, James was quickly able to broker peace. He believed in the Divine Right of Kings – that is, he was answerable only to God – a position that did not go down well with the English parliament, particularly when he levied new customs duties without their consent after they had refused to fund his extravagances. James ruled for long periods without reference to parliament unless he needed money. In 1605 the most famous of anti-James conspiracies occurred: the Gunpowder Plot. Sir Robert Catesby led a group of conspirators who wanted the king to grant tolerance to the Catholics. They proposed to blow him up at the state opening of parliament, but one of their number warned a Catholic peer of their plans. The cellars were searched and the conspirators executed.

James's homosexual tendencies and fondness for favourites earned him little respect. One, Robert Carr, was made Earl of Somerset, but he was accused of murdering his secretary and fell from the king's favour. Carr was succeeded by George Villiers, soon made Duke of Buckingham, who was a strong influence on James's foreign policy. James was anxious to secure alliances through the marriage of his children. An attempt to marry Charles, Prince of Wales, to the Spanish Infanta foundered but he fared better with his daughter Elizabeth who married Frederick the Elector Palatine. However, when Frederick accepted the crown of

Bohemia in 1618, he angered the Holy Roman Emperor who believed it was his. This disagreement marked the beginning of the Thirty Years War and James was reluctantly pressed towards war with Spain until parliament refused him funds.

James bequeathed the nation a number of legacies in the books he wrote and in particular by commissioning a translation of the Bible into English. The Authorised Version was published in 1611.

Charles I (r. 1625–49)

Born 1600
Died 1649
Married 1625, Henrietta Maria (daughter of Henry IV of France). Nine children.

Charles – affectionately but not very tactfully known to his father as 'Baby Charles' even into his youth – was a sickly child and a small man, standing only 5 feet 4 inches tall. He had a tendency to hero-worship, first it was his charismatic older brother Henry, whose death in 1612 shocked the realm, and then his father's favourite, Buckingham, with whom, in 1623, Charles set off on a wild adventure with the aim of securing his betrothal to the Spanish Infanta. They rode to Madrid to pay court in person but returned defeated and humiliated. If nothing else, Charles's experience of the magnificent Spanish palaces made him resolve to become a great patron of the arts and, in this, he would abundantly succeed.

Charles's marriage to Henrietta Maria, daughter of the King of France, began badly. Charles, who had by now inherited the throne, was cold and repressed and Henrietta Maria, a child of only fifteen when she arrived in London, was jealous of Buckingham. In fact, Buckingham ran the country, at a large deficit, until his assassination by a discontented officer in 1628. Charles was distraught at his friend's death but there was one positive outcome for him. As the queen comforted him, they fell in love.

Charles was politically inept and inflexible. He lacked the skills for intrigue and had no understanding of his realm or his people. He tried to rule England without parliament for twelve years, raising money by exploiting various ancient rights of the crown, but this policy, added to a growing sense that the king and his Catholic wife were straying from the true Protestant path, built up a huge bubble of resentment that eventually burst. Parliament, recalled at last to provide the impoverished king with money, revolted and open warfare ensued. Charles's cause went well until parliament took to the field with a professionally trained and fanatically motivated force, Oliver Cromwell's New Model Army. Defeated and captured, Charles proved intransigent in negotiations and the parliamentary generals lost patience with him. Tried for treason, he was condemned and publicly beheaded in Whitehall on 30 January 1649. He is the only British monarch to have died by judicial process.

Charles II (r. 1660–85)

> **Born** 1630
> **Died** 1685
> **Married** 1662, Katherine (daughter of John IV, Duke of Braganza). Three children (all stillborn).

Charles spent virtually the first ten years of his reign in exile, trying to raise the forces to overwhelm Oliver Cromwell, 'Protector of the Realm', so he could take up his rightful position as King of Scotland and England. However, it was not until Cromwell's death in 1658 that his ministers could negotiate his return.

Crowned in 1660, Charles's attention was immediately taken up with foreign affairs. He allied himself with the French against the Dutch, but the conflict came to nothing because of trouble closer to home. In 1665 the plague took its toll on England followed in 1666 by the great fire of London which eradicated the rat-infested city slums where the disease festered. In 1670, Charles concluded the secret Treaty of

Dover with the French in which he agreed to support them against Holland and to declare his Catholicism in exchange for financial support.

A strong anti-Catholic feeling in the country meant that Charles was made to agree to the Test Act which barred all public offices to Catholics. In 1678, Titus Oates spoke of a plot to kill Charles and make his younger brother James king, thereby restoring Catholicism to the country. As a result, various notable Catholics were executed and an attempt was made to exclude James, an avowed Catholic, from the throne.

Charles was known as the 'merry monarch'. He was a great patron of the arts and sciences, an energetic sportsman and womaniser. He had a string of mistresses, including the Duchess of Portsmouth and Nell Gwynne, and fathered thirteen illegitimate children. He converted to Catholicism on his deathbed but nevertheless was buried in Westminster Abbey.

James II (r. 1685–88); also James VII of Scotland

Born 1633
Died 1701
Married
(i) 1659, Anne Hyde (daughter of the Earl of Clarendon). Eight children. Died 1671.
(ii) 1673, Mary (daughter of the Duke of Modena). Twelve children.

At the Restoration, James, Charles II's younger brother and a staunch Catholic, returned to England from exile. He was made Lord Admiral and fought in the Dutch wars but was made to relinquish office in 1673 when the Test Act was passed.

Few wanted a Catholic king in Scotland or England, so when he acceded to the throne, there was plenty of opposition. Two rebellions were immediately orchestrated, one led by the Earl of Argyll in Scotland and the other by James, Duke of Monmouth, in England. Both were swiftly scotched and the leaders executed. James thus began his reign of terror, taking little notice of parliament and determined to restore Catholicism to England. In 1688, a Declaration of Indulgence dropped the restrictions on Catholics and Non-conformists. Seven bishops protested vociferously. As a result they were taken to the Tower and tried for seditious libel. All were found innocent and released.

All this might have been tolerated in the knowledge that the two heirs to the throne were his Protestant daughters, Mary and Anne, from his first marriage, but when the queen gave birth to a boy who would inevitably be brought up Catholic, the country's worst fears were realised. (It was widely believed that the baby was a changeling smuggled into the royal bedchamber in a warming pan.) The 'Immortal Seven', made up of the Bishop of London and six statesmen, petitioned William of Orange, the husband of James's daughter Mary, to restore Protestant England and protect his wife's inheritance. William duly arrived with his troops at Brixham and marched on London. James recognised his lack of support and abdicated before fleeing to France, dropping the great seal of England into the Thames as he went.

James was determined to win back his crown and set up a court in exile. With French support, he travelled to Dublin where he held a parliament and governed, but he was defeated by William at the Battle of the Boyne in 1690. He retired to France where he spent the rest of his life plotting against England.

William III (r. 1689–1702) and Mary (r. 1689–94); also William IV of Scotland

Born 1650
Died 1702
Married 1677. Three children (all stillborn).

After the Glorious Revolution (so called because no blood was shed) when William had been key to the flight of James II, Mary was reluctant to take the throne. She was not a political animal and preferred to take second place to her husband. After two months' deliberation, they became joint sovereigns, accepting a parliamentary Declaration of Rights which detailed how James II had abused his royal position. This was later incorporated in the 1689 Bill of Rights. Their authority was also restricted by the First Mutiny Bill which forbade any monarch to keep an army in time of peace without parliament's consent.

There were pockets of dissension in the kingdom which William was able to deal with. He defeated James at the Battle of the Boyne and became known as King Billy. He was as successful in the Scottish highlands, but in 1692 was responsible for the Glencoe massacre in which his troops annihilated the Macdonald clan. Thereafter his popularity was severely damaged.

William was not particularly interested in governing England but he *was* determined to keep the French out of Holland. His wars were concluded in 1697 with the signing of the Treaty of Ryswick by England, Holland, France and Spain. As a result of the fighting, 1694 saw the establishment of the Bank of England to provide necessary finance.

After Mary died of smallpox in 1694, William ruled alone. As before, his attention was focused abroad, most particularly on the Spanish succession, and he left the running of the country to parliament. In 1701, the Act of Settlement ensured that if neither William nor Anne (James II's other daughter) had children the throne would pass to a Protestant, Sophia, Electress of Hanover, granddaughter of James I.

In 1702, his horse tripped on a molehill and William broke his collarbone. The resulting complications killed him. He was buried in Westminster Abbey.

Anne (r. 1702–14)

Born 1665
Died 1714
Married 1683, George (son of King Frederik III of Denmark). Nineteen children (14 stillborn).

When Anne inherited the throne she was overweight and prone to gout. She had to be carried into her coronation and was unable to stand because of the pain. Her taste for a drop of brandy earned her the nickname 'Brandy Nan'. She had fallen out with her sister, Mary, because of her friendship with the Churchills. Sarah Churchill and Mary had known each other since childhood, and when Sarah's husband, John, was accused of plotting against William, Anne refused to turn against them. Mary was furious and never spoke to Anne again.

Her reign was dominated by the War of the Spanish Succession which raged over France's and Austria's competing claims to the Spanish throne. The fighting had begun while William was on the throne but continued until 1713 when Britain and France signed the Treaty of Utrecht. It was John Churchill who became England's hero, fighting successfully in numerous campaigns. Anne honoured him with the title Duke of Marlborough and gave him a royal estate in

Anne

Oxfordshire which he named Blenheim after his splendid victory there. In 1711 Anne dispensed with his and his wife's services after Sarah allied herself with the Whigs.

Most significantly, the 1707 Act of Union united Scotland and England, transferred the Scottish parliament to Westminster and Anne became the Queen of Great Britain, France and Ireland. Her reign was also notable for the development of a two-party political system and the rivalry between the Whigs and the Tories dominated parliament. In 1708, to Anne's chagrin, the Whigs won a majority in the House of Commons but this was overturned in the 1710 general election by the Tories. During Anne's reign trade developed and the country prospered.

Anne died of a stroke and was buried in Westminster Abbey. She had become so fat that her coffin was almost square.

The Hanoverians, 1714–1910

 George I (r. 1714–27)

Born 1660
Died 1727
Married 1682, Sophia Dorothea (daughter of George William, Duke of Brunswick-Luneborg-Celle). Two children. Annulled 1694.

The 1701 Act of Settlement made sure only a Protestant could inherit the throne. Then the closest Protestant heir was Sophia, Electress of Hanover but her death in 1714 meant the throne passed to her son, George. Unable to speak English, George was not a popular king. His marriage to Sophia Dorothea had not worked and her affair with Philippe von Koningsmark had ended with his disappearance and her life imprisonment, banned from remarriage and forbidden to see her two children. It was rumoured that von Koningsmark had been murdered and his body hidden under the floorboards of the Electoral Palace. George was widely known to have a mistress whom he may have secretly married.

George was not much welcomed when he arrived in London for his coronation. The Scots liked him even less and in 1715, the first Jacobite rebellion took place at Braemar led by the 'Old Pretender', James II of Scotland. It was easily quashed.

George's lack of English meant that his son, another George, acted as his interpreter and representative at parliamentary meetings, and as regent during the king's absences abroad. They fell out in 1717 and the prince's role was taken over by Sir Robert Walpole, leader of the Whig party and 'prime' minister since 1714. Since the king was often abroad and decisions were taken from his hands, this was the real beginning of the government by cabinet that we have today. Walpole was ousted from his post in 1717 so that George could use two weaker members of his cabinet, Sunderland and Stanhope, to agree to his desire for an alliance with Holland and France against Russia. But Walpole sided with the king's son who, with his influential wife Caroline, tried to thwart the king's scheming. Before long George realised he was safer with Walpole on his side so he brought him back to the cabinet as First Lord of the Treasury after the South Sea Bubble crisis. The South Sea Company had been established in 1711 with the encouragement of numerous investors who all lost their money when the company crashed in 1720. Several government ministers were implicated but it was Walpole who had the skill to save the court from scandal. From then on, George took a back seat in government, preferring to spend half the year in Hanover. It was there that he died of a cerebral haemorrhage in 1727 and was buried.

 ## George II (r. 1727–60)

Born 1683
Died 1760
Married 1705, Wilhemina Charlotte Caroline (daughter of John Frederick, Margrave of Brandenburg-Ansbach).

George II

There was no love lost between George I and his son George II who had never forgiven his father for his cruel treatment of his mother. George and his wife Caroline came to London when his father was crowned and set themselves up in what was almost a rival court at Leicester House. There life was fun and the flirtatious Caroline, who had a keen interest in politics, surrounded them with powerful supporters, most notably Robert Walpole.

George did not learn from his relationship with his father. He and Caroline both loathed their first son, Frederick Louis, Prince of Wales. They regarded him as a philanderer and considered his liking for sport and the arts to be misguided. As a result he loathed them and frequently sided with the opposition. They successfully orchestrated his marriage to Princess Augusta of Saxe-Gotha, then virtually ostracised her. The marriage produced nine children before Frederick's death in 1751.

When George came to the throne, Walpole remained his first minister and curtailed the king's enthusiastic plans for campaigning abroad. However, when Queen Caroline died, Walpole's influence began to decline (he resigned in 1742).

In 1739 England became involved in a war against Spain after Captain Robert Jenkins claimed his ear had been cut off by Spanish coastguards operating in the Caribbean. In 1740, England's forces were joined with those of France in the War of the Austrian Succession. In 1743 George himself led his troops into battle at Dettingen, Bavaria, the last reigning king to do so; 1756 marked the beginning of the Seven Years War with France.

Trouble was also brewing in Scotland where James, the 'Young Pretender', itched to regain the English and Scottish crowns. He led the Jacobite rebellion of 1745 which was finally crushed the following year by George's son, William, Duke of Cumberland, at the bloody Battle of Culloden. Afterwards, the Jacobites were treated very harshly and the movement was all but wiped out.

George III

Generally, George's reign was prosperous and saw an expansion of the empire, thanks particularly to victories in India and Canada. His popularity had grown since he first took the throne. A martyr to constipation, he died from a heart attack on the lavatory in his apartments in Kensington Palace. He was buried beside his wife in Westminster Abbey.

 George III (r. 1760–1820)

Born 1738
Died 1820
Married 1761, Sophia Charlotte (daughter of Charles, Duke of Mecklenburg-Strelitz).
Fifteen children.

George's father Frederick, Prince of Wales, died in 1751 so he knew from the age of thirteen that he would eventually succeed his grandfather, George II. He did so at the age of twenty-two, making him the first Hanoverian monarch to be born and brought up in

England, to speak fluent English and to feel culturally at one with his realm. Yet he was immediately persuaded by his prime minister, the Earl of Bute, that he should look for an alliance with Germany, turning away from his youthful infatuation with Lady Sarah Lennox to marry Sophia Charlotte, two weeks before their joint coronation.

George was a Tory, deeply imbued with the traditions of England. He respected the authority of parliament but wished to reclaim what he thought of as the crown's legitimate share of power and to weaken the Whigs who had been so dominant over the past forty-five years. He was also a deeply religious man. At first he was unlucky in his prime ministers. In an aggressively confident and nationalistic England, the Earl of Bute, with his Scottish ancestry, was unpopular and in 1763 he resigned, though not before he had successfully ended the Seven Years War with France. George made do with a succession of stop-gap prime ministers until, in 1770, he appointed Lord North, a man chiefly remembered for having lost the American War of Independence and the majority of England's North American colonies. George felt the loss keenly and, despairing of a government he could work with, considered abdication. But he decided to soldier on with the new Whig administration, although its main thrust was to wrest even more power from him. Then, in a tense general election in 1783, Pitt the Younger carried the day, beginning an unbroken twenty-one years of Tory rule.

The middle period of George's reign was stable and prosperous, marred only by the unhappy relationship between the king and his son (later George IV), and by his first attack of porphyria whose symptoms resemble madness. Despite the extreme treatments meted out by his doctors, George recovered and was declared of sound mind in 1789. In 1801, Pitt, having achieved the Act of Union with Ireland, tried to go one step further by putting through an act which emancipated Catholics. The king believed that signing any such act might result in forfeiting the crown. Pitt felt his only course of action was to resign. Meanwhile, in France, Napoleon was strengthening his power base. In 1804 Pitt was returned to power and was instrumental in dictating England's role in the Napoleonic wars.

His last ten years saw the king in a terrible decline; his son George acted as regent from 1811. All sorts of causes have been blamed for his 'madness', from despair at the loss of the American colonies to the twentieth-century diagnosis of porphyria. He was moved to Windsor Castle where he lived, blind and suffering, wandering his rooms with long grey hair and beard in his purple dressing gown, until his death in 1820.

George IV (r. 1820–30)

Born 1762
Died 1830
Married
(i) 1785, Maria Anne Fitzherbert (daughter of Walter Smythe). No children.
(ii) 1795, Caroline Amelia Elizabeth (daughter of Charles II, Duke of Brunswick). One daughter.

George IV

George III doted on his young son George, but like all Hanoverian father–son relationships it was soon to sour. Though well-grounded in the arts and sciences, the young prince had a penchant for wine, women and song and indulged himself whenever the opportunity arose. He deliberately allied himself with the Whigs to irritate his father but his charm made him the darling of London society.

He had a succession of mistresses until he met the staunch Catholic Maria Fitzherbert who would not succumb, insisting instead on marriage. In 1785, he obliged in secret, flouting the 1772 Royal Marriages Act which meant the marriage was null and void in the eyes of the law if not of the Church. George knew that if he married a Catholic he would forfeit his right to the throne under the Act of Settlement, so he went as far as getting his friend George Fox to deny the marriage to parliament. His extravagances were legendary, running up huge debts that the king and parliament were forced to pay off. However, in exchange they insisted he formally marry Caroline of Brunswick. The pair loathed each other on sight but in 1794 they married, George relying on drink to get him through. He allegedly spent the night asleep by the fireplace. However, nine months later, Caroline gave birth to their daughter Charlotte.

The highlight of his years as regent was Wellington's victory over Napoleon at the Battle of Waterloo in 1815 which marked the end of the Napoleonic Wars. Otherwise he ran a lavish court, rich in pleasure and intrigue. On his accession to the throne in 1820, he tried to get parliament to pass an act barring Caroline from the throne. Despite their refusal he barred her from attending the coronation ceremony and she died only weeks later.

On taking the throne, George broke any promises he may have made to his Whig friends and kept his father's Tory ministers in power. He tried to oppose the power of the prime ministers during his reign but was routinely unsuccessful, no more so than in 1829 when the Catholic Emancipation Act was passed, freeing Catholics from previous restrictions and allowing them public office. His love for spectacle and pageant never faded: he made the first Hanoverian tour of Ireland and Scotland in great pomp and splendour, and oversaw a huge building programme which most notably included the Brighton Pavilion.

George spent the last years of his life as a recluse at Windsor; the years of overeating and drinking had taken their toll.

 William IV (r. 1830–37)

> **Born** 1765
> **Died** 1837
> **Married** 1818, Adelaide (daughter of George, Duke of Saxe-Meiningen).
> Six children (four stillborn).

William was the third son of George III and had no expectations of the throne. Unlike his elder brothers, he was never trained for kingship but instead was sent to sea at the age of thirteen. From able seaman he rose through the ranks, seeing action in Gibraltar and the West Indies, and was best man at Nelson's wedding in 1787. He was finally made Admiral of the Fleet in 1811. When he retired from active service in 1785, he settled down with a popular actress of the day, Mrs Jordan, and over the next twenty years they had ten children. He left her abruptly for reasons unknown and she died of a nervous and physical breakdown in France.

When Princess Charlotte, daughter of George IV and heir to the throne, died, the race was on for the sons of George III to produce heirs. William found a devoted wife in Princess Adelaide but sadly their two daughters died in their youth. He took no interest in the arts or sciences though he did install a library at Windsor because he felt it was the proper thing for a castle to have. When it came to the coronation, William insisted on a simple affair that was to cost a tenth of his brother's. He increased the popularity of the royal family by visiting London, Brighton and Windsor but his role in politics was minimal. By dissolving parliament, he tried to prevent the passing of the Reform Bill that would greatly diminish the powers of the monarchy. However, he was forced to recall it and in 1832, against his better judgement, he supported Earl Grey and asked the Tory peers to abstain from voting. One hundred of them did and the bill was approved. This was a significant step towards modern democracy and cleared the path for other social reforms.

At the age of sixty-four, William was the oldest monarch to come to the throne and he was upset by what he saw as an overturning of the established order. He recognised that his was principally a caretaking role until his niece Princess Victoria came of age. There was no love lost between him and the Duchess of Kent, Princess Victoria's mother, and he was determined she should not become regent. Fate was on his side and he died from pneumonia and cirrhosis of the liver one month after Victoria's eighteenth birthday.

Victoria (r. 1837–1901)

> **Born** 1819
> **Died** 1901
> **Married** 1840, Albert (son of Ernst I, Duke of Saxe-Coburg-Gotha). Nine children.

Victoria was the daughter of Edward, the fourth son of George III, and Princess Victoria of Saxe-Coburg-Gotha, later the Duchess of Kent. Her father died when she was only eight months old and his role in Victoria's life was largely taken by her uncle Leopold, the widower of Princess Charlotte.

When Victoria acceded to the throne, the popularity of the monarchy was at a low, not helped by a scandal at court during the first year of her reign when she forced one of her mother's ladies-in-waiting to undergo a pregnancy test, believing her to have had an affair with her mother's chief adviser. The test revealed the woman to be a virgin suffering from advanced cancer of the liver.

Victoria

Apart from her uncle Leopold, Victoria placed greatest faith in her first prime minister, Lord Melbourne, until she married Prince Albert in 1840. The royal couple were young, in love, and valued their privacy over the social life of the court. Victoria bought Osborne House in the Isle of Wight and Balmoral House in Scotland to provide them and their nine children with retreats well away from the public gaze. Albert was a man of culture and taste with a strong moral sense. His influence over his wife extended into government policy-making, particularly with regard to social welfare, and slowly the working-man's lot began to improve with the passing of education and public health acts.

In 1851, it was Albert's initiative that led to London's Great Exhibition where exhibitors paraded industrial products from all over the world. Meanwhile, Victoria's relationships with European monarchs promoted peace in Europe. Her reign saw England's involvement in the Crimean War against Russia, the Indian Mutiny and non-involvement in the American Civil War.

When Albert died of typhoid in 1861, aged forty-two, Victoria was devastated. She went into mourning and withdrew from her duties. Eventually she found comfort in the companionship of John Brown, a servant at Balmoral, which raised many eyebrows. She kept in touch with the government of the country through her prime ministers, interceding in foreign affairs only to promote peace or neutrality. She had to deal principally with two prime ministers, Gladstone and Disraeli. In 1886, Gladstone introduced the Home Rule Bill aimed to restore an Irish parliament in Dublin. Victoria's adamant opposition to the bill split the Liberal Party. However, she got on better with Disraeli who ensured his place in her heart by making her Empress of India in 1876.

When Victoria died in 1901, the British Empire was at its height, the monarchy had regained its popularity and was linked through marriage to many of the royal houses of Europe. Social reforms had changed the face of England and the idea that monarchy had influence rather than power was fully established.

Edward VII (r. 1901–10)

Born 1841
Died 1910
Married 1863, Alexandra Caroline Marie Charlotte Louise Julie (daughter of Christian IX of Denmark). Six children.

Edward was the second son of Queen Victoria and Prince Albert. Christened Albert Edward, he was popularly known as Bertie. He rebelled against his strict upbringing and was known for his sense of humour and enjoyment of the good life. He loved travelling, horse-racing, sailing, hunting and even the new pursuit of motoring. Like his Hanoverian predecessors, he enjoyed a string of mistresses, much to the disapproval of his mother. Relations with Queen Victoria were strained by his hedonistic behaviour and she never forgave him for an incident involving a young actress which she believed contributed to his father's early death. He was married swiftly after that to Princess Alexandra who was commendably tolerant of her husband's ways. Despite his involvement in two major scandals, the country loved him and welcomed the relief he provided from the sobriety of his mother's reign. In 1862 he bought the Sandringham estate as a retreat for his family.

Victoria excluded him from almost all domestic political duties, preventing him from seeing diplomatic and political papers but allowing him to perform public ceremonies and travel abroad on state visits. Eventually, when he became king in 1901, he took most interest in his role as ambassador overseas, visiting relatives, maintaining peace in Europe and helping to achieve the 1904 Entente Cordiale between France and England. As a result, he became known as Edward the Peacemaker.

Edward had inherited his father's social conscience and was a philanthropic man. During his reign, the Liberals introduced a number of social reforms, including the introduction of pensions, national insurance and the recognition of trade unions.

Conservative at heart, though, Edward opposed the move towards women's suffrage.

In the last year of Edward's reign, the Chancellor of the Exchequer, Lloyd George, introduced a budget which proposed higher taxation of the wealthy to fund social reform. There was an outcry. The bill was thrown out by the House of Lords and the government demanded that the king should create more Liberal peers to give the party a majority. Edward tried to find a way to compromise but became ill with chronic bronchitis before the matter could be resolved. He died at the height of the crisis, passing it on to his son George V.

The House of Windsor, 1910–

 George V (r. 1910–36)

> **Born** 1865
> **Died** 1936
> **Married** 1893, Mary Augusta Louise
> (daughter of Franz, Duke of Teck).
> Six children.

As the second son of Edward, George did not expect to attain the crown and had chosen a naval career. This ended when his elder brother Albert died in 1892. The following year he married Albert's fiancée, Mary, and began to be prepared for his future role. Unlike his father, he had nothing of the playboy in him though he enjoyed sporting rather than intellectual pursuits (his favourite hobby was stamp-collecting). The year following the coronation, he and Mary travelled to India where they were crowned emperor and empress.

George reluctantly resolved the political crisis

inherited from his father by referring the matter to a committee. A general election ensured a Liberal majority and the acceptance of Lloyd George's budget. His reign was dominated by the outbreak of the First World War in 1914. He made no secret of his feelings about his cousin, the German Kaiser, whom he held directly responsible for it and supported the government's decision to declare war on Germany after its invasion of Belgium. He visited the troops abroad regularly to maintain morale. In the face of extreme anti-German feeling, he changed his family name from Saxe-Coburg to Windsor.

After the war, George was immediately involved in the resolution of the Irish conflict over the Home Rule Bill. In this, as in everything that followed, he proved himself a fair and conciliatory ruler. The 1916 Easter Rising and execution of the rebels had only increased nationalist fervour. George encouraged Lloyd George towards a peaceful solution so in 1921 Ireland was finally partitioned into the Irish Free State and Ulster. At home, the first Labour government was voted in under

Ramsay MacDonald in 1924, somewhat to the king's alarm. Rumours of their connections with communism meant their success was short-lived and they were followed by Baldwin and the Conservatives. In 1926 George had to check the extreme measures proposed by Baldwin to end the General Strike. By the end of the decade the country was in the grip of a world depression and the king actively encouraged the formation of a national government of all three parties in 1931. Nineteen thirty-two saw the first royal Christmas broadcast, subsequently an annual tradition.

In 1935 the country celebrated the royal Silver Jubilee. The following year, George contracted a respiratory infection and died at Sandringham. Mary died in 1953.

 Edward VIII (r. 1936)

Born 1894
Died 1972
Married 1937, Wallis Simpson. No children.

Edward VIII

Edward VIII was never cut out to be a king. From his youth he made plain his dislike for ceremonies of state and had little interest in state affairs. He was refused active service during the First World War and his royal activities were limited to representing his father in visits abroad. The king disapproved of his womanising lifestyle, and hoped his son would marry and settle down, ready to assume his royal duties. Edward showed no sign of obliging until he met the American Mrs Wallis Simpson who lived in London with her second husband. By 1935 he was passionately in love with her and, by the time he acceded to the throne, he had persuaded himself that he would marry her. The idea that the king would marry a twice-divorced woman was inconceivable to the Church, to the government and to his mother and provoked a massive constitutional crisis. Edward was adamant: either their marriage went ahead or he would abdicate. In December 1936 he abdicated in favour of his astounded brother Bertie (George VI). The next day he broadcast a moving speech to the nation and sailed immediately for France where he married Wallis Simpson a few months afterwards. In 1937, he was given the title Duke of Windsor by his brother George

VI. The fact that Mrs Simpson was denied an honorific was an irritant for the rest of his life.

The couple lived in self-imposed exile in Paris until the Second World War broke out. An ill-advised visit to Germany in 1937 earned him the reputation of being a Nazi sympathiser though his keenness to serve Britain ensured his appointment as Governor of the Bahamas until the end of the war. Until his death from cancer in 1972, they lived in Paris enjoying a busy social whirl. Wallis Simpson succumbed to senile dementia but lived on in their house until she died in 1986.

George VI (r. 1936–52)

Born 1895
Died 1952
Married 1923, Elizabeth (daughter of Claude George Bowes Lyon). Two children.

The second son of George V, Albert Frederick Arthur George or 'Bertie' had no expectations of succeeding to the throne. He joined the Royal Navy in 1913 and fought in the First World War until, for health reasons, he joined the Royal Naval Air Service. In 1920 he was made Duke of York and began civic duties on behalf of his father. In 1923 he married Elizabeth Bowes Lyon. They led a settled family life with their two daughters, the princesses Elizabeth and Margaret, though occasionally they would have to make official visits abroad.

The abdication crisis was totally unexpected. Bertie had three weeks to prepare himself for the role of king. He took the name George V and took his brother's place at the scheduled coronation. When he took the throne, he admitted he had never even seen a state paper, but he was a conscientious man and set about his task with determination. His first prime minister was Neville Chamberlain and they shared the view that the threats from Italy and Germany should be dealt with peaceably. This led to the signing of the Munich Agreement in 1938. However, when it became clear that a declaration of war was the only way to prevent the fascist advance through Europe, George immediately supported this change in direction. His role in the war was as a figurehead to encourage morale and to ensure the support of the commonwealth countries. After Chamberlain's resignation, George had to overcome a slightly chilly start to forge a firm bond with his new prime minister, Winston Churchill.

After the outbreak of war, the two princesses were sent to Windsor but the king and queen remained in London, sharing the hardships of their subjects. Buckingham Palace sustained a direct hit and in 1942 the king's younger brother, the Duke of Kent, was killed in active service. They frequently visited the worst-hit areas of the East End, showing Londoners they weren't alone. George also went abroad to boost the morale of the troops and established the George Cross and the George Medal for acts of bravery.

After the war, a Labour government was elected under Attlee. The king continued his policy of advising not instructing but made it perfectly clear that he felt their nationalisation programme went too far. He continued to make his royal visits, notably to South Africa and Rhodesia in 1947. That same year he saw the British withdrawal from India. In 1951, he opened the Festival of Britain to celebrate post-war Britain.

George's health deteriorated rapidly after an operation for arteriosclerosis in 1948 and a brush with lung cancer in 1951. Eventually he died in his sleep after a day shooting rabbits at Sandringham and was buried in a newly constructed chapel at Windsor.

 ## Elizabeth II (r. 1952–)

Born 1926
Married 1947, Philip (son of Prince Andrew of Greece and Denmark). Four children.

Elizabeth is the first sovereign of the television age. Her coronation in 1953 was watched by millions. Over the years, she has used television to bring her closer to her subjects, though the media have gradually become less of a blessing, turning the family into something resembling characters from a soap opera, and being openly critical of their behaviour. Media intrusion has even been blamed for the death of Princess Diana, the wife of her son and heir Prince Charles, in 1997.

The empire, which was already being dismantled when Elizabeth came to the throne, gave way to the British Commonwealth. She has dedicated herself to it with great determination, holding regular meetings and undertaking state visits to the member nations to foster good relations.

Nowadays the monarchy is not regarded as instrumental in the country's political fortunes. Britain's involvement in the Suez Crisis (1956) or the Falklands conflict (1982) has been the government's responsibility not the queen's.

Despite her enthusiastic championing of the concept of a royal family and the continuation of the folksy idea that it is a 'family firm', her own children, as they grew to adulthood, have been Elizabeth's biggest problem. Three out of their four marriages have ended in divorce and they are routinely held up to ridicule in the tabloid press. The queen's own rectitude seems a relic from an earlier age, and her lack of the popular touch, in contrast to Princess Diana's public image and the popularity of her own mother, has occasionally made her seem inflexible and aloof.

Nevertheless, Elizabeth II takes the long view. Still queen of many countries in the Commonwealth, her position may seem unfashionable and perhaps redundant, but in the long term she will receive credit for her sheer tenacity and relentless hard work.

SCOTLAND

When the Romans left Britain, they left a divided country. Just as England consisted of seven rival kingdoms warring for control, so Scotland was being fought over by the Picts, the Scots and the Angles. By 848, Kenneth Mac Alpin had united the Picts and the Scots into a country he called Alba with its political capital at Forteviot and its spiritual capital at Dunkeld. Very little is known about Mac Alpin but there is no doubt that he began the process of uniting the country we now know as Scotland. There followed countless attacks to be repelled from the English and Viking armies, not forgetting the rivalries between those who believed they had a claim to the throne within Scotland itself. It was not until the reign of Malcolm II (r. 1005–34) that the boundaries of Scotland became recognisable as they are today. He was victorious against the English and Vikings, bringing the kingdom of Lothian under his rule, shortly followed by an alliance with the kingdom of Strathclyde. Until that point the crown had been passed to the next most suitable candidate, but Malcolm knew of the principle of primogeniture exercised in England. He did his best to secure the throne for his grandson Duncan by attempting to murder all the descendants of Kenneth III (997–1005).

 ## Duncan I the Gracious (r. 1034–40)

Born c.1001
Died 1040
Married Sybilla (daughter or sister of Siward, Earl of Northumbria). Three or four children.

Duncan was not the wise king portrayed by Shakespeare. In 1040 he led a hopelessly mismanaged expedition against the English at Durham from which he had to retreat. He delayed again when it came to mounting an attack on the Vikings in the north, leaving their leader Thorfinn time to regroup his defences. Duncan was forced to flee into Moray where he was killed in battle against Thorfinn's ally, Macbeth.

Macbeth

 Macbeth (r. 1040–57)

Born 1005
Died 1057
Married 1033, Gruoch (widow of Gillecomgain).
No children.

Macbeth was far from the scheming tragic figure depicted by Shakespeare. He had a legitimate claim to the throne as the grandson of Malcolm II of Scotland and ruled wisely and well. The first fourteen years of his reign mark a stable period in Scotland's history, so secure that he even mounted a pilgrimage to Rome. However, in 1054 he faced a major threat from Duncan's son, Malcolm, who had been brought up in the court of Edward the Confessor. With the English king's support and the leadership of his uncle, Siward of Northumbria, Malcolm confronted Macbeth's army at Dunsinnan. Macbeth may have been defeated but he continued to rule from Moray while Malcolm took Strathclyde. After three years of civil war, Macbeth was ambushed and murdered.

Lulach the Fool (r. 1057–58)

Born 1031
Died 1058
Married Finnghuala (daughter of Sinhill,
Mórmaer of Angus). Two children.

Lulach was Macbeth's stepson and Kenneth III's
great-grandson whom the Scots supported over Malcolm
because of his Gaelic upbringing. His short rule consisted
of nothing but conflict which was resolved by his ambush
and murder by Malcolm III's supporters.

 Malcolm III Canmore (r. 1057–93)

Born 1031
Died 1093
Married
   (i) c.1060, Ingibiorg (widow of Thorfinn, Earl
   of Orkney). Three children.
   (ii) c.1069, Margaret (daughter of Edward
   Atheling). Eight or more children.

Malcolm III Canmore

Despite the fact that he had been brought up in the Saxon court of Edward the Confessor, it was the English who were to prove Malcolm III's downfall. With the death of his ally, Siward, Northumbria was taken over by Tostig of Wessex, brother of Harold Godwinson. Tostig's unpopularity brought instability to the region that made it a target for both the kings of Scotland and England. Malcolm invaded five times, eventually to be killed with his eldest son in a trap in 1093. Hostilities against William I of England were constant, although Malcolm was compelled to recognise him as overlord in 1072. Malcolm tried to seal an alliance with the Scandinavians by marrying Thorfinn's daughter. After her death he married Edward Atheling's daughter, Margaret, a deeply religious woman who did her best to reform the Scottish Church and bring it in line with Rome. They had a strong partnership which did much to stabilise Scotland. Malcolm had brought various ideas from the English court with him and managed to establish the rule of primogeniture as well as introducing feudalism. His rule marked a fundamental shift in Scotland from the traditional Gaelic ways to an acknowledgement of more modern beliefs.

Donald III Bane (r. 1093–94 [deposed]; 1094–97)

Born 1033
Died 1099
Married, unknown. One child.

Malcolm's eldest son was killed with him in 1093, so the throne was seized his younger brother, Donald, who drove any Norman or Saxon supporters from the country. In retaliation, Malcolm's son, Duncan (the eldest from his first marriage), who had spent much of his life as a hostage in the English court, fought back with the support of William II. He drove Donald out and became Duncan II (r. 1094). His reign was short-lived and he was defeated seven months later at the Battle of Monteith. Donald then joined forces with another of Malcolm's sons, Edmund (r. 1094–97), and they split the kingdom between them, Donald ruling north of the Clyde and Edmund to the south. This arrangement lasted until another of Malcolm's sons, Edgar (r. 1097–1107), was declared King of Scotland by William II of England. Edgar deposed Donald and Edmund, imprisoning and blinding Donald and exiling Edmund to Montacute Abbey where he became a monk. Edgar ruled peaceably from Edinburgh. He ceded the Hebrides (including the holy island of Iona) to Magnus III of Norway rather than fight for them. He acknowledged his fealty to the English throne and agreed to his daughter marrying Henry I of England.

He was succeeded by his sons, Alexander I the Fierce (r. 1107–24) and David. However, Alexander insisted on his supremacy, granting his brother lands in Strathclyde and the borders. Like Edgar, he paid homage to Henry I and strengthened ties by his marriage with Henry I's illegitimate daughter. A younger son of Malcolm III and Margaret, he continued his mother's work in anglicising the Scottish Church and encouraging monastic orders. As his rule went on he retrenched himself in Scone, carrying out an impressive programme of castle-building and winning over the support of the highlanders.

David I the Saint (r. 1124–53)

Born 1084
Died 1153
Married 1113, Matilda (daughter of Waltheof, Earl of Northumberland). Four children.

David was the youngest son of Malcolm III and Margaret. He was under ten when both his parents died and was brought up in the Norman court of Henry I. His marriage to an English widow gave him the earldoms of Northampton and Huntingdon which made him uniquely both Scottish king and Norman baron. On his accession to the Scottish throne, David continued to develop the relationship between traditional and modern systems. He developed the system of feudalism, giving lands to various Norman families such as the de Brus, the de Bailleuls and the Fitzalans who settled in lowland Scotland. In exchange they were loyal to the king and paid him taxes. He established a parish system throughout the country and founded several royal burghs (e.g. Edinburgh, Selkirk, Berwick and Perth) which became major trading centres with a system of self-government entrusted to the town guilds. He encouraged and funded the establishment of new monasteries in southern Scotland, instituted a strong system of coinage, revised the judicial system and redrew the administrative map of Scotland. He tried to extend the Scottish border further south, battling for Northumberland and Cumberland in the name of Matilda, the daughter of Henry I, whom he supported over Stephen for the English crown. However, he was defeated by Stephen at the Battle of the Standard in Northallerton in 1138 but was granted the earldom of Northumberland in exchange for his loyal support.

Both David's sons died before him, so his crown was inherited by his twelve-year-old grandson Malcolm IV the Maiden (r. 1153–65). The highland chieftains were displeased by Malcolm's apparent loyalty to Henry II, particularly when he accompanied him on a mission to Aquitaine. This led to a series of rebellions, all of which Malcolm effectively quashed. He was a religious man who never married, so when he died aged only twenty-three he left no direct heir to the throne. Instead, his brother William the Lyon (r. 1165–1214), only a year his junior, took over. He was determined to regain control of Northumberland which had been lost to England under Malcom IV. His attempt to reclaim it only led to the Treaty of Falaise in 1173 by which he virtually handed Scottish independence to Henry. He then concentrated his efforts on bringing the rebellious Scottish highlanders under control, consolidating the government of the country. In 1189, Richard I of England desperately needed finance for the third crusade so essentially sold Scotland back to William, making him king of all Scotland. He married late but fathered four sons to continue the dynastic line.

William's son, Alexander II the Peaceful (r. 1214–49), maintained ruthless control over the north of Scotland despite rumblings of dissent. He joined the Norman barons who rebelled against King John and was one of the signatories of the Magna Carta at Runnymede in 1215. He strengthened his relationship with King Henry III by marrying his sister, although he refused to recognise the authority of the English king over Scotland.

In 1238 it was agreed that, in the absence of a direct heir, the Norman Robert de Brus would accede to the throne. This enraged the highlanders who took up arms. That same year, however, Alexander married for a second time and had a baby son, Alexander III the Glorious (r. 1249–86) who was only eight when he came to the throne. Three years later he married the daughter of Henry III and, like his father, refused to acknowledge the authority of the English king over him. In 1263 he launched a successful attack on the Vikings in the Western Isles, thus creating the

Scottish boundaries that still exist today. In 1286 his horse stumbled on a cliff and he fell to his death.

All Alexander's children had died before him so the throne fell to his granddaughter Margaret, Maid of Norway (r. 1286–90). However, she was only four and living in Norway with her father the king. The constitution was in turmoil so the six 'Guardians' who had been elected by the Scottish parliament asked for help from Edward I of England. He supported Margaret's right to the throne and proposed she marry his son. However, she died while sailing to Scotland before any of this could happen.

After her death, there was a brief interregnum while the Scots once more appealed to Edward I for help in choosing one of the thirteen claimants to the throne. He chose John Balliol (r. 1292–96), a descendant of David I. He was an ineffectual leader, regarded by Edward as a puppet-king. Balliol paid homage to Edward, and Scotland was called upon to provide funds for English wars abroad. Balliol finally rebelled when told to support Edward against Philippe IV of France, both financially and by joining his troops. Instead he joined forces with the French king, but his attempt at independence was futile and he was forced to surrender in 1296 when Edward's troops invaded and massacred the garrison at Berwick. John Balliol was deposed the following month and sent to the Tower of London. Edward, now known as Hammer of the Scots, was triumphant and removed the Stone of Scone, the seat on which the Scottish kings were crowned and the symbol of Scotland's nationhood, to Westminster Abbey.

A second interregnum followed, during which Edward ruled from England, leaving his representatives as administrators in Scotland. He underestimated the Scots' grit and determination and faced a serious challenge from William Wallace (r. 1297–98). Son of a Clydesdale landowner, Wallace began by conducting guerrilla warfare against the English castles and garrisons. Then he joined with Andrew Murray and together they led their men to overthrow the English at

Stirling Bridge in 1297. Wallace had no wish to be king, so was declared Guardian of Scotland. His rule was short, though, for it did not take long for Edward to rally his forces and defeat Wallace at Falkirk the following year. Wallace escaped and disappeared for several years until he was betrayed by one of his men in 1305, captured near Glasgow and hung, drawn and quartered.

 ### Robert I the Bruce (r. 1306–29)

Born 1274
Died 1329
Married
  (i) 1295, Isabella (daughter of Donald, Earl of Mar). One child.
  (ii) 1302, Elizabeth (daughter of Robert de Burgh, Earl of Ulster and Connaught). Four children.

Robert was the Earl of Carrick and a claimant to the throne thanks to his ancestral connection with David I. Originally a supporter of Edward I, he changed his allegiance to William Wallace. However, at Wallace's death, Robert made peace with Edward and was appointed one of four regents to rule Scotland while Edward fine-tuned the arrangements for ending independent government there. Robert killed one of his co-regents, John Comyn, in an argument in a Dumfries church, then declared himself king with the support of his countrymen. Immediately Robert was driven into hiding on Rathlin Island where, legend has it, watching a spider spinning its web inspired him never to give up the struggle. He returned to wage an uncompromising battle for an independent Scotland. The tide had turned in his favour with the accession of Edward II, a far weaker king than his father. The decisive victory came when Robert besieged Stirling castle in 1314 and, two days later, routed Edward II's army at the Battle of Bannockburn despite the fact that his army was a fraction of the size of the English.

In 1320 the Declaration of Arbroath, proclaiming Scottish independence, was signed by the Scottish barons and submitted to the pope. However, the English ignored the declaration and continued fighting until Edward III came to the throne in 1327 and signed the Treaty of Northampton, formally recognising Robert as King of Scotland. In 1329 he died of leprosy.

 David II (r. 1329–71)

Born 1324
Died 1371
Married
(i) 1328, Joanna (daughter of Edward II of England). No children.
(ii) 1364, Margaret (daughter of Sir Malcolm Drummond). No children. Divorced.

David was Robert the Bruce's only son. He was only five years old when his father died but was already married to the daughter of Edward II, and remained so for the next thirty-four years. The year after they were jointly crowned, Edward Balliol (son of John Balliol) invaded Scotland with the support of Edward III. He drove David into exile and was crowned king. Three months later he was deposed and David restored to the throne. Edward III responded immediately by invading Scotland, defeating the Scots at Halidon Hill. David was exiled to France and although restored to the throne in 1336, he did not return until 1341 when Balliol was finally expelled.

In 1346, David joined forces with France against the English and led his troops south. He was defeated at Neville's Cross and taken to the Tower of London where he was imprisoned for eleven years until his release under the Treaty of Berwick, whereby he was forced to pay Edward a massive ransom for his freedom. The second part of his reign was relatively quiet, marked by the restoration of the royal finances and the dedication to maintaining Scottish independence. He died suddenly after two marriages without leaving an heir.

Robert II (r. 1371–90)

Born 1316
Died 1390
Married
 (i) 1336, Elizabeth Mure of Rowallan. Ten children.
 (ii) 1355, Euphemia (daughter of Hugh, Earl of Rose). Four children.

Nephew of David II and grandson of Robert the Bruce, Robert was fifty-five when he came to the throne and well past his prime; in fact, he was known as 'Auld Blearie' because of his bloodshot eyes. He immediately named his son John, Earl of Carrick, as his successor. As Robert became senile, John took over but neither man was fit to govern the country or able to control the growing violence and disorder. When John was incapacitated by a kick from a horse, the reins of government were passed to his brother Robert.

Robert III

 Robert III (r. 1390–1406)

Born c.1337
Died 1406
Married c.1366, Annabella (daughter of Sir John Drummond of Stobhall). Seven children.

On the death of his father, John, Earl of Carrick, confusingly changed his name to become Robert III. He had already proved he was unfit to rule during his father's reign so his brother Robert retained his position of control. In 1393, Robert III decided to take power back into his own hands, with disastrous results: the country collapsed into virtual anarchy, divided between the highlanders and the lowlanders, and poverty was rife. In 1398 Robert III's brother, Robert, was made Duke of Albany and his son, David, became Lieutenant of the Realm. David was as inept as his father and in 1401, on the instructions of the Duke of Albany, he was flung into prison and left to starve to death. In 1406, Robert III arranged for his other son James, heir presumptive, to be sent to France both for his education and safety. However he was captured by pirates and taken to the court of Henry IV of England where he was held hostage for eighteen years. Robert III pined to death and asked to have these words on his coffin: 'Here lies the worst of kings and the most wretched man in the whole kingdom.'

 James I (r. 1406–37)

> **Born** 1394
> **Died** 1437
> **Married** 1424, Joan Beaufort (daughter of John, Earl of Somerset; great-granddaughter of Edward III). Eight children.

For the first eighteen years of his reign, James was held hostage in London. In his absence, Scotland was ruled by his grasping uncle Robert, Duke of Albany, and then his son Murdoch. By 1424 when James returned to Scotland with his wife, John of Gaunt's granddaughter, the state of the country had deteriorated. James was an educated man, well-acquainted with court affairs and immediately devoted himself to the task of restoring stability to his country. He removed power from the nobles by imprisoning many of them and instituted tax and judicial reforms. He summoned all the leaders of the troublesome highland clans to a meeting in Inverness where he arrested them all. He introduced firm legislation, developed trade and revived good relations with France, marrying his daughter to the Dauphin. His ruthless attitude made James many enemies and in 1437 he was assassinated during an attempted coup. The assassins may have succeeded in getting rid of the king, but their plan for installing a new one was foiled; they were captured and horribly executed.

 James II (r. 1437–60)

Born 1430
Died 1460
Married 1449, Mary (daughter of Arnold, Duke of Gueldres). Seven children.

James was only a child when his father was murdered, so the responsibility for running the country was immediately contested by three rivals, Sir William Crichton of Edinburgh castle, Sir Alexander Livingstone of Stirling castle and the Douglas family. Matters were exacerbated by a notorious dinner at Edinburgh castle, hosted by James, where the young Earl of Douglas and his brother were arrested, sentenced in a mock trial and executed. Thereafter the Douglas family joined with Livingstone in deadly enmity against the under-age king and Crichton. The 1440s were subsequently a period of great civil unrest until James came of age in 1449. That same year he married Mary, niece of the Duke of Burgundy, establishing his kingship on a par with other European courts. Throughout his youth, he had been trained for his role as king so he knew to deal swiftly and surely with his enemies, crushing the Livingstones immediately. When William Douglas refused him total allegiance, James stabbed him to death. Incensed, his brother James Douglas immediately transferred his allegiance from the Scottish to the English king, Henry VI. James II reacted by launching a series of campaigns against Douglas territories in the south, finally subduing them in 1455 and keeping his kingdom whole. Over the next few years, James systematically reduced the power of the great Scottish families, extended the legislation introduced by his father, and founded Glasgow University in 1450.

James was fascinated by the new artillery that had helped him in his victories, but when he lit a cannon just before a planned assault against the English at Roxburgh castle, it exploded and killed him. Another of his cannons, Mons Meg, can still be seen at Edinburgh castle.

James III (r. 1460–88)

Born 1452
Died 1488
Married 1469, Margaret (daughter of Christian I of Denmark and Norway). Three sons.

Like his father, James was only a boy when he came to the throne. His mother was regent during a period dominated once again by a noble family keen to augment their power, namely the Boyds of Kilmarnock. When James took full authority, he had the Boyds put on trial for treason. They were sentenced to death.

A truce with England was in place so James devoted the early years of his reign to patronising the arts and encouraging learning. The aristocracy condemned James for what they saw as his persistent toadying to the English and his over-preoccupation with the arts, and turned to his two brothers, Alexander and John, for leadership. They were tried for treason in 1479 and imprisoned. John died in obscure circumstances, but Alexander escaped and fled to France.

By 1482 the Anglo-Scottish truce had broken down because of border disputes and Alexander proclaimed himself Alexander IV with the support of Edward IV of England. Alexander invaded from the south and James was briefly imprisoned in Edinburgh castle. Berwick was returned to the English. With the death of Edward IV, the English army withdrew their support and James was freed. He continued to rule much as before until, in 1488, open rebellion broke out once more, the nobles putting up the king's eldest son (James IV) as their figurehead. James III led his troops to meet them at Sauchieburn where he was defeated. He escaped, only to be assassinated a few hours later.

 James IV (r. 1488–1513)

> **Born** 1473
> **Died** 1513
> **Married** 1503, Margaret (daughter of Henry VII of England). Six children.

Guilty at his role in his father's death, James IV wore an iron belt every day of his life, to which he added an extra weight each year. When he first came to the throne he immediately pulled the country round under his control, achieving a peaceful relationship with his nobles and settling differences with those who had supported his father. The highlands were in turmoil but he managed to effect a peace of sorts despite some clan resentment. Though renowned as a warrior, he thoroughly reviewed the administrative and judicial procedures of the country. He encouraged the arts and sciences: the first printing press was set up in Edinburgh under his patronage; Aberdeen University was founded in 1495; the Royal College of Surgeons was founded in 1506. He was interested in architecture and promoted renovation and rebuilding at both Edinburgh and Stirling castles. He was a talented linguist, devoutly religious, and pursued many interests such as hunting, music and sport (though he banned football in 1491 to encourage people to take up archery!). He undertook a massive expansion of the navy, his pride and joy being the construction of the *Great Michael*, the biggest warship in the world.

James saw the advantages of promoting peace with England but found himself cornered into supporting Perkin Warbeck, a pretender to the English throne.

Together they invaded Northumberland but their lack of success and Warbeck's irritation with James led to their separation. Instead, James agreed the 1503 Treaty of Perpetual Peace with Henry VII whereby he married Henry's twelve-year-old daughter Margaret, securing peace between the countries, extending Stuart influence and safeguarding England against the might of James's navy. However, the peace was to last only ten years. When Henry VIII invaded France in 1513, James had no choice but to support Scotland's old ally and invade England. The two armies met at Flodden Field. The Scottish army was decimated, the king and many of his nobles slain.

James V (r. 1513–42)

Born 1512
Died 1542
Married
   (i) 1537, Madeleine (daughter of François I of France). Died 1537.
   (ii) 1538, Mary (daughter of Claude I, Duke of Guise-Lorraine). Three children.

James V was only seventeen months old when his father James IV died at Flodden Field. For the next fifteen years the country was governed by a regency until, in 1528, James dispensed with the office and ruled himself.

James's mother, Margaret Tudor, initially assumed the role of regent, though she was not popular with the Scots because she was Henry VIII's sister. However, she quickly forfeited her role and the care of her child by her marriage to Archibald Douglas, Earl of Angus, in 1514. The Scottish parliament asked John, Duke of Albany (nephew of James III and next in line to the Scottish throne after James V) to return from France to fulfil the role. Margaret then changed sides and supported Albany against her estranged husband. The two-way struggle was further complicated by the fact that Albany was a French sympathiser and wanted Scotland to ally with France once again, while Angus had pro-English sympathies. Eventually Albany returned to France in 1524, never to return. Angus immediately stepped in and kept the young king prisoner in Edinburgh castle.

James V

James escaped to Stirling castle in 1528, the year he came of age. Angus sought refuge in England while Margaret Tudor married Henry Stewart, Earl of Methven. They became close advisers to James until Margaret fell from favour, accused of betraying court secrets to her brother Henry VIII.

James immediately consolidated his country by crushing the uprising of nobles on the borders and in the highlands. He also signed an Anglo-French peace treaty in 1528 which was to last five years. As a king, he was particularly unpopular with his nobles because of the brutal way he curbed their powers and because of the high taxes he demanded from them. He established the Courts of Justice in 1532 and reinstituted regular meetings of parliament. He firmly rejected Henry VIII's Protestant policies and courted the pope who agreed to pay him an annuity and give James's five sons Church appointments which would keep them in pocket.

In 1537, James married Madeleine, daughter of the French king, but she died shortly afterwards. Keen to maintain a marital alliance with France, he married Mary of Guise-Lorraine. They were heartbroken by the early deaths of both their baby boys in 1541. By 1542, relations with England had worsened, leading to an inevitable confrontation at Solway Moss. However, the Scottish turnout was feeble, James having failed to rally support, and many of the nobles deserted him in his hour of need. The English victory was a walkover. James died a month later, just after the birth of his daughter, Mary.

Mary, Queen of Scots (r. 1542–67)

Born 1542
Died 1587
Married
   (i) 1558, François (son of Henri II of France). No children. Died 1560.
   (ii) 1565, Henry, Lord Darnley (son of Matthew Stuart, 4th Earl of Lennox). One son. Died 1566.
   (iii) 1567, James, Earl of Bothwell. Twins (stillborn).

Mary, Queen of Scots

Since Mary was only a week old when her father died, a regent was appointed though she remained in her mother's care. Soon after Henry VIII attempted to secure her betrothal to his son, Edward. The Scottish parliament immediately annulled it which inflamed hostilities between England and Scotland. The Scottish were defeated in battle at Pinkie in 1547 and Mary was sent to France for safekeeping. The ensuing years of the regency were marked by French and English antagonism. In 1558, Mary married François, the French dauphin who became King of France the following year. Protestant Scots repudiated the idea of having a French king and rebellions broke out across the country, with the English supporting them against the French. In 1560, the Treaty of Edinburgh called for the withdrawal of French and English troops from Scotland. That same year, François died, leaving Mary as Queen of Scotland and dowager Queen of France with her own lands and income.

Mary returned to Scotland where, although a Catholic herself, she tolerated Protestantism. The early years of her reign saw her re-establish the power of the monarchy and its finances. Despite her ambitions to have her claim to the throne recognised by Elizabeth I, ambitions which could have been secured by a suitable marriage, she married her cousin Henry, Lord Darnley. She filled her court with her favourites which antagonised many nobles. Her court secretary, David Rizzio, was suspected of being her lover and was murdered by Darnley in her chamber. Shortly after the birth of their son, James VI, Darnley was killed under mysterious circumstances at Kirk o' Field, just outside Edinburgh. The Earl of Bothwell was tried and acquitted of his murder. Mary then shocked the nation by marrying Bothwell immediately after his hasty divorce from his wife. The nobles were outraged. The couple fled but were captured and Mary was forced to abdicate in favour of her son James.

She escaped to England where she threw herself on the mercy of her cousin, Elizabeth I, who had no choice but to imprison her. Mary had many Catholic supporters who were prepared to conspire to set her on the English throne. Eventually, in 1586, she was implicated in the Babington plot against Elizabeth. Anthony Babington and his co-conspirator, John Ballard, were executed. Mary was tried and found guilty of treason. Elizabeth delayed signing her death warrant for as long as she could but eventually Mary was beheaded at Fotheringay Castle.

 James VI (r. 1567–1625)

Born 1566
Died 1625
Married 1589, Anne (daughter of Frederick II of Denmark and Norway). Nine children.

James never saw his mother again after she was deposed. His coronation, a few days later, was modest and extremely poorly attended. Over the next years there was a succession of four regents, the most notable of whom was the Earl of Morton from 1572 to 1580.

Morton was a committed Protestant ruler who kept the country together by keeping good relations with Elizabeth I and defeating any Catholic plots to reinstate Mary, Queen of Scots. Towards the end of this period, James befriended Esme Stuart, a cousin of Lord Darnley's. He was involved in the overthrow of Morton and rumoured to be promoting the Catholic cause. This alarmed the Protestant faction so much that in 1582 William Ruthven, Earl of Gowrie, held James hostage after a day's hunting near Perth, refusing to release him until Esme Stuart was banished.

James took over the reins of government when he was seventeen years old. He reduced the power of the controlling nobility and established a more moderate court made up of his favourites who supported his wish to form an alliance with England and to control the power of the Protestants. He believed in the Divine Right of Kings which made him answerable only to God. This directly contradicted Andrew Melville, leader of the Presbyterians, who claimed that all men, including the king, were equally answerable to God. Such a doctrine gave the Presbyterian Kirk (Church) considerable authority which James checked by making strategic appointments to the General Assembly. So great was his desire not to upset Elizabeth that he barely objected to the execution of his mother, Mary, and refrained from involvement in England's hostilities with Spain. In 1586 he concluded a treaty with Elizabeth which recognised him as her successor.

In 1589 James married Anne of Denmark. Her arrival in Scotland was postponed because of the weather so he sailed to collect her and they were married in Oslo. When James returned it was to discover that the Earl of Bothwell was suspected of being involved with a group of lords who were practising witchcraft in an attempt to bring about James's downfall.

Bothwell was banished but returned to cause more trouble until his support finally waned and he was exiled for good. Threats of rebellion from the northern

Catholic lords who maintained sympathy with the Spanish were decisively quashed. In 1600 an attack on James's life by the Gowrie family was thwarted.

By 1603, James had united the kingdom and made the power of the monarchy dominant. He was only too ready to succeed Elizabeth when she died and left for London a few days later, returning to Scotland only once in the next twenty-two years of his reign. (See James I of England.)

From this point, Scotland and England were ruled by one monarch seated in London with separate governments in each country. In 1707 the Act of Union formally united the two countries and relocated the seat of Scottish government to London.

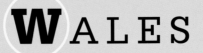

In the 5th century, after the Roman legions had departed, Britain was gradually divided into the three principal areas of Wales, England and Scotland. The construction of Offa's Dyke in the 8th century was the first clear delineation of a boundary between England and Wales. At that time Wales was divided into a number of kingdoms which, thanks to the practice of partible inheritance (i.e. the equal division of an estate between sons), were often subdivided further still. It was a land of multiple kingships complicated by territorial battles, border disputes, internecine rivalries and family quarrels. Any attempts to unify the nation were made even more difficult by the often dramatic and hostile landscape.

By the 9th century, many of the smaller kingdoms had merged to form two principal kingdoms: Gwynedd in the north (Snowdonia and Anglesey), and Deheubarth (Dyfed and Seisyllwg) in the south; with the smaller Morgannwg (Gwent and Glywysing) in the south-east and Powys in the east. It was only at this time that the few rulers who could claim to be kings of Wales appeared.

The first was Rhodri Mawr (Rhodri the Great), the third king to be known as 'Great', after Alexander and Charlemagne. He ruled Gwynedd from the death of his father in 844, Powys from the abdication of his uncle in 855 and Seisyllwg after the death of his brother-in-law in 872. Together these formed the greatest unified part of Wales to be ruled by one king for years. His success as a king was to show to his people that they could act together as a force against invasion. He invested them with a national identity and belief in their might. Under his leadership they successfully fought a number of battles against the Vikings who attacked the Welsh coast. In the east, they successfully defended the borders of Powys against incursions from the kingdoms of Mercia and Wessex. Rhodri's reign lasted for over thirty years until he was killed in 878 fighting against Mercia.

Rhodri's grandson Hywel Dda (Hywel the Good) is the next Welsh ruler of influence. He was given Dyfed in

904 and Seisyllwg in 920 when they combined to become Deheubarth. In 942 Deheubarth was united with Gwynedd and Powys on the death of his cousin in battle. Hywel was a regular visitor to the British court and in 928 made a pilgrimage to Rome. He sensibly recognised that a conciliatory approach towards the English was a wiser policy than aggression. Through his travels he saw the benefits of an organised system of administration and jurisdiction with the result that he summoned a conference at Whitland made up of representatives from every parish. Together they thrashed out the first codified legal system for Wales (Cyfraith Hywel Dda) which was to give a lasting cohesion to Wales even after his death. Uniquely in the history of Wales, he issued his own coinage to give another form of unity to his people. His rule was marked by his diplomacy and justice; he was the only ruler to have the epithet 'Good' attached to his name. After his death, his lands were once more split up and anarchy ruled again.

Gruffydd ap Llywelyn

It was not until the time of Hywel's great-great-grandson Gruffydd ap Llywelyn (1000–63) that Wales regained political unity. Gruffydd was a fearsome war-mongerer who seized power over Gwynedd and Powys in 1039 after the murder of its ruler. He moved on to engage in several battles aimed at overthrowing Deheubarth but the opposition was fierce and, although the losses were staggering, he was thwarted by equally determined rulers. Meanwhile, he also succeeded in gaining territories east of Offa's Dyke by allying himself with Alfgar of Mercia. He at last won victory over Deheubarth in 1055, killing the ruler in battle and claiming the land as his own. Now he could call himself King of Wales and set up a court at Rhuddlan. The English recognised his authority and, in 1057, Harold Godwinson, Earl of Wessex, agreed a treaty with him in which Gruffydd declared his loyalty to Edward the Confessor. He none the less continued his activities along the Welsh border and, in 1062, Harold mounted a surprise invasion. Gruffydd escaped by sea. The following year Harold tried again and this time cornered him inland, giving his enemies the chance to kill him. After his death his lands, like Hywel Dda's before him, were divided up and Wales was never again wholly united under a single sovereign.

In 1066, William the Conqueror took the throne of England and proceeded to secure the frontier with Wales by installing his barons in castles along the Welsh Marches. It was not until the birth of Llywelyn ap Iowerth (Llywelyn the Great) in 1173 that Wales saw another leader of real stature uniting most of the country. He rose rapidly to power in Gwynedd by taking advantage of family squabbles and annexing or claiming the separate parts as his own. By 1202 he had successfully reunited the kingdom. He continued to campaign over the next years until Powys (1208) and Deheubarth (1216) were under his rule.

He was a shrewd man who gladly came to terms with King John of England, agreeing that while John was overlord of Wales, Llywelyn would rule the country.

Dafydd ap Llywelyn

In 1205, he married John's daughter and even supported him fighting against William of Scotland. Proclaiming himself Prince of Wales in 1210 was a less shrewd move and King John retaliated by invading Gwynedd and forcing Llywelyn to retreat. Fortunately, John's attention was deflected by problems with the pope and the barons, giving Llywelyn a chance to reassert his power. In 1216 the Treaty of Worcester confirmed him as Prince of Wales with authority over the other Welsh rulers. He achieved much in his lifetime, reorganising and revising the political and legal administration of the country as well as establishing peaceful relations with England and Rome. So determined was he that his work should not be undone after his death, he substituted the law of primogeniture for the law of partible succession and named his son Dafydd as his heir.

Within a year of his succession, Dafydd ap Llywelyn (r. 1240–46) had provoked the anger of Henry III who invaded Wales, insisting on the return of lands captured by Llywelyn after the Treaty of Worcester. Henry's trump card was to take Dafydd's half-brother, Gruffydd, and nephew, Owain, as hostages. Dafydd knew that if he crossed Henry, the English king would support Gruffydd's cause as Prince of Wales against him. For a while things were quiet. Then Gruffydd died and Dafydd resumed his hostilities against the English. Henry III raised an invasion force but Dafydd died before the battle was concluded.

Henry III swept through the country, subduing insurrections and signing the Treaty of Woodstock in 1247 in which Dafydd's successors, Llywelyn ap Gruffydd (Llywelyn the Last) and his two brothers lost all the land of Gwynedd east of the River Conway. But Llywelyn was far from satisfied and he determined to regain the lost territories. He began by defeating his two brothers at the Battle of Bryn Derwin in 1255 which gave him sole authority over Gwynedd. Then, supported by other native princes, he began to claim the rest of Wales taken by Henry. In 1258, under the Peace of Montgomery, Henry accepted Llywelyn's homage as

Llywelyn ap Gruffydd

Prince of Wales. However, Llywelyn's hold on his country was tenuous, particularly because his lack of an heir meant that there were several warring factions with their eye on the title.

Things really began to fall apart with the accession of Edward I to the English throne. From the beginning, Llywelyn seemed to go out of his way to antagonise him, refusing to pay him homage or the payments due under the Treaty of Montgomery, proposing marriage to the daughter of Simon de Montfort, the rebel baron, and strengthening fortifications. By 1276, Edward I had invaded Wales. It took just one year before Llywelyn was forced to submit. The humiliation of the Treaty of Aberconwy stripped him of everything he had gained ten years earlier, leaving him with only the heartland of Gwynedd and the now meaningless title of Prince of Wales. From then on an uneasy peace was maintained until Llywelyn's brother Dafydd attacked Hawarden Castle in 1282. Llywelyn had no choice but to side with his brother despite his sworn loyalties to Edward I.

Inevitably, the English king's reaction was swift and merciless and by the end of the year Llywelyn was dead.

The battle raged on for four more years until Dafydd finally surrendered. The 1284 Statute of Rhuddlan was drawn up to define the terms under which Wales was to be ruled by England. Power was removed from the local princes and their lands became shires administered by a governor-general. To the anger of the Welsh, Edward proceeded to give his son the grace and favour title of Prince of Wales.

Although Llywelyn ap Gruffydd was effectively the last king of a unified Wales, Owain Glyndwr, a Marcher Lord and a descendant of the princes of Powys and Deheubarth, declared himself Prince of Wales in 1400 and led a nationalist rebellion against the English. By this time, the Welsh had become resentful of English tyranny which was crippling their economy and readily lent Glyndwr their support. After four years of struggle, Glyndwr called a parliament at Machynlleth and had himself crowned Prince of Wales with his French,

Owain Glyndwr

Scottish and Castillian allies in attendance. A year later he held his second parliament in Harlech. By this stage he had reached an alliance with Edmund Mortimer (an English turncoat who had married Glyndwr's daughter) and Henry Percy, Earl of Northumberland. Together they devised a plot to overthrow Henry IV and divide the country between them. However, Glyndwr's support was weakening in the face of the English offensive. The final disaster came in 1408 when the castles of Harlech and Aberystwyth were captured and Glyndwr's family was taken prisoner. Glyndwr himself was forced into hiding. This was the last gasp of Welsh independence against the English crown. No one knows what became of Glyndwr but his name has become synonymous with the notion of Welsh independence. The punitive anti-Welsh laws imposed by Henry IV as he attempted to control the uprisings stayed firmly in place until Henry VII came to the English throne. His Welsh ancestry gave hope to the Welsh people and he didn't entirely disappoint them, removing some of the land restrictions imposed after Glyndwr's insurgency and appointing the Welsh nobility to senior posts and to territories in Wales, at last diminishing the power of the Marcher Lords. In 1536 and 1543 the Acts of Union finally set the terms by which Wales was no longer a separate province but part of the English sovereignty.

IRELAND

A Different Idea of Kingship

Irish ideas about kingship were always associated with magic and myth. In legendary times the Side, a fairy race, were said to have inhabited the land which was a paradise of ease, peace and plenty. Then came the invasion of the first men, bringing plague, war and kings.

Early Irishmen are named in the myths as Fir Bolg who ruled for aeons until challenged by a new tribe, the Tuatha de Danaan. The Fir Bolg king Eochaid, who is said to have championed the first Irish legal system, was killed by the king of the Tuatha de Danaan, Nuada. The latter possessed a prophetic Stone of Destiny which bellowed like an elephant when kicked by the true king. In spite of this talisman, his people were in turn supplanted by a new wave of invaders, the 'Spanish' Milesians, who drove the Tuatha de Danaan underground. In the old stories the Milesian brothers Eber and Eremon ruled between them, but fell out over the prized possession of the Hill of Tara. Eremon, who won Tara, thereby became High King.

A Different Idea of Kingship

Tara (about 40 miles north-east of Dublin in modern Co. Meath) is just one of the more spectacular of the remains left by pre-Celtic Neolithic and bronze-age peoples – standing stones, forts and burial mounds – that show that they were great builders and monument-makers, implying they had good social and political organisation, although little is known about how they were grouped or governed. Nevertheless, the iron-age Celts or 'Milesians', who probably did originate in Iberia and arrived in the middle of the 1st millennium B.C., found much to wonder at.

The High King, or *ard-rí*, of Tara was a prestigious ceremonial title but only once in the long Celtic domination of the country was it established as something more, and then but briefly. In the parts of western Europe conquered or influenced by Rome, the notion of a divinely sanctioned ruler and law-giver, granting land in return for service, imposing his will and his justice, had been adopted by the invading tribes and was endorsed by Christianity. But Ireland had been virtually unaffected by imperial Rome and the people came very late to the idea that a king's power might be God-given. Nor, in a cattle-based economy, did they consider land as the basis of wealth. Their chiefs drew authority from being heads of their families and tribes in an economy based on herds of cattle. The laws were not theirs to make, nor was the land theirs to distribute, and these attitudes persisted even as the 'Roman' ideas about kingship began to spread under the influence of the Church, and then the Normans, between the 8th and 11th centuries.

Celtic Ireland had been a politically fragmented land of 80–150 small and feuding tribes, or *tuatha*, which were themselves made up of a number of self-regulating family groups or *fine*. Although there were no large-scale political structures, there was a common law (the *brehon* law) and this held sway in most places. The power centre of the *tuath* was its chieftain and his army, which was in more or less continuous movement. The frontiers of their territories shifted. Herds moved or were raided.

A Different Kind of Kingship

Conflicts with neighbouring tribes arose and were resolved through battle or negotiation. Prior to the coming of Christianity and its monasteries, there were no permanent settlements of any size.

The tribes were hierarchical and the strong men who led them were chosen from within their own class. Under this caste were others of nobles, warriors, *áes dána* (intellectuals, poets, etc.), freemen (craftsmen, smallholders) and, at the bottom of the heap, slaves. It was a pre-literate culture yet the *brehon* law, which regulated all levels of the social order and prescribed how wrongs were to be redressed, was passed down very precisely by word of mouth through designated 'lawyers', the *brehon*. It was based on a system in which wrongs were put right either by vendetta – family-against-family and *tuath*-against-*tuath* – or by restitution according to a scale laid down by the *brehon*. The king was not necessarily the fount of justice and there was no developed notion of punishment.

There were differences in the degree of power

wielded by the kings. Lesser tribes commonly submitted to greater ones and here and there larger political units began to appear. These *cuigi*, or provinces, eventually evolved into the five kingdoms of Munster, Leinster, Meath, Ulster and Connacht, but they had no fixed boundaries and large *tuatha* continued to exist within them, retaining varying degrees of autonomy. The spread of Christianity, after St Patrick arrived in *c.*432, gave Ireland its first concentrated and settled centres of population, the monasteries. It also brought literacy and instigated the gradual decline of the *brehon* law. But the Irish still resisted 'Roman'-style political centralisation and before 800 the individuals who crop up in the island's history are rarely the kings. They are the church leaders like Patrick himself, Finnian, Brendan, Columba and Brigid.

Gradually the *cuigi* did develop as kingdoms, with their own ruling dynasties. In the north the Uí Néill held the regional kingships for many centuries, and in the south the Eóganachta, based at Cashel, did likewise. The

A Different Kind of Kingship

Church encouraged this and Irish kings were among the first to be consecrated by bishops at their coronation.

The political pattern was traumatically affected by successive waves of Viking invasion in the 9th and 10th centuries, but eventually the Vikings, too, were absorbed into a new order in Ireland. Their trading posts such as Dublin, Wexford, Waterford and Cork were the first towns in Ireland and Dublin became an important kingdom in its own right.

The Uí Néill Kings, 5th to 10th centuries

The true origins of the Uí Néill – Ireland's greatest political dynasty – are overlaid by many legends sponsored by their own propagandists. It is clear, though, that by the 7th century they dominated the kingdoms of Meath and Ulster and by the 9th they were pushing into Leinster, where they laid claim to the (still largely symbolic) position of High King of all Ireland. But the Uí Néill were not a unitary dynasty led by a single figure. They split and split again, until there were several distinct branches, two of which had long-term importance: one based at Derry and Donegal, the other at Tara. Only a few individuals are worth a mention here.

 ### Niall Noigíallach (Niall of the Nine Hostages)

5th century

Known mostly through legend, Niall extended his

kingdom by conquering the territory of the **Airgialla** around modern Armagh, in Ulster. The 'Nine Hostages' suggests his domination over nine subsidiary *tuatha*, who yielded hostages to him in token of their submission, a practice which continued for many centuries.

 ## Laoghaire

The son of Niall of the Nine Hostages and a contemporary of St Patrick, Laoghaire welcomed the saint and was converted by him at Tara in 432.

 ## Máel Sechnaill I

Died 862

He made strong claims to be High King and certainly achieved overlordship over many *tuatha*. He also took on the marauding Vikings with great success, killing 700 at Skrean in 848 and sacking the new Viking trading post of Dublin.

Niall Glúndab of Tara

Died 919

Niall had some success in containing the Viking menace in Leinster, but was killed in battle with the Vikings of Dublin who had established a strong kingdom of their own along the eastern seaboard, with important links with their kinsfolk in northern England.

Donnchad of Tara

Donnchad was Niall's successor, who fought back, burning Dublin and the Viking ships more than once.

Domnall Uí Néill (r. 956–80)

An aggressive ruler, originally from the northern branch of the Uí Néill, he tried to consolidate his dynasty's power into a single unitary Uí Néill kingdom, taking over the seat at Tara from his power base in Derry and Donegal and establishing garrisons in Meath.

Máel Sechnaill II (r. 980–1022)

Son of Domnall, he was the last of the old-style Uí Néill kings of Tara. He inherited his father's dominions and, though he lost the high kingship to Brian Boru, regained it after the Battle of Clontarf.

The Eóganacht Kings, 7th to 10th centuries

Claiming descent from one Eógan, of whom nothing is known, this dynasty controlled Munster from the 7th to the 10th centuries, with their seat at the ancient Rock of Cashel in modern Co. Tipperary. Of their kings perhaps only Feidlimid mac Crimthainn (820–47) stands out. A learned man, Feidlimid was a bishop-king but he was also a ruthless ruler who plundered the monasteries of his enemies the Uí Néill and waged vigorous war on them.

Other Early Dynasties, 7th to 8th centuries

 Uí Dunlaínge

Kings of Leinster in the 8th century, based in the Liffey valley and allied to the church in Kildare.

 Uí Chennselaig

Originally challenging the Uí Dunlaínge in northern Leinster, they were pushed south until finally carving out a kingdom for themselves in the 7th century in modern Co. Wexford.

 Uí Fiachrach

One of the dominant powers in Connacht, they claimed kinship with the Uí Néill. The most famous king was Guaire Adni (d. 663) who has come down in the chronicles as a model of good governance and saintly character.

Uí Briúin

This aggressive dynasty ruled most of Connacht by 725 and maintained its regional power for several hundred years.

Uí Bríainne (O'Briens) of Dál Cais

The kingdom of Dál Cais, whose heartlands straddled the waterway of the Shannon river in North Munster, was the successor power to the Eóganacht in Munster as a whole, thanks to the aggressive expansionism of the Uí Bríainne dynasty, especially Mathghamain and his brother Bríainne Bóroime (Brian Boru). Mathghamain began by allying himself with the Munster king Cellachán of Cashel but within ten years he had turned against his ally and captured the Rock of Cashel itself, forcing Cellachán to submit to him. In 967 he defeated the Vikings in their stronghold of Limerick, with much plunder. After considerably more military success, he was assassinated nine years later on the orders of an alliance of his enemies, led by the Viking Christian King of Limerick, Ímar.

 ## Brian Boru (r. 976–1014)

Born c.932
Died 1014

The greatest of all the Irish chieftain-kings was the second son of Cennétig, King of Dál Cais and North Munster. He assumed the kingship in 976 after his brother and dealt swiftly and ruthlessly with the assassins, slaughtering Ímar and his family despite their having sought sanctuary at the monastery of Scattery Island. Brian then pursued the goal of becoming High King of Ireland in fact as well as in theory with single-mindedness and outstanding political and military skill. He took his seat at Cashel and made war on the Uí Niálls in Connacht, Meath and finally, in 991, Leinster. In 997 he was strong enough to make a favourable peace with Máel Sechnaill II in which they agreed to divide Ireland, with Máel yielding Leinster to Brian. Brian took up his seat at Tara in 1002 and for the next few years he systematically subdued the whole country. In 1005 he entered the apostolic city of Armagh, offering gold at the high altar of St Patrick's Cathedral, recognising the archbishop as Primate of All Ireland and laying formal claim to be himself recognised as 'the Emperor of Ireland'.

Although now very aged, he assembled a large army at Clontarf in 1014 to crush the Viking kingdom of Dublin. Too old to fight himself, his forces were led by his son Murchad, while Brian observed from his pavilion on high ground above the battlefield. His forces swept the Vikings from the field but he himself was killed by one of the defeated enemy who, coming across Brian's tent in his flight, cut him down. The king never knew that Murchad too had been killed in the fighting.

The Seven Kingdoms

Politically, seven great provincial Irish kingdoms now developed which, for most of the 12th century, were constantly at war with each other. Although the office of High King continued to be held, by election (or grudging agreement) among the provincial kings, no one was now capable of giving the office the unifying power of Brian Boru. At the same time, in their own provinces, the kings increasingly resembled the feudal rulers of mainland Europe. They tended to hold land centrally and distribute it as they wished, to dispense their own laws and justice and to pass their crowns from father to son. They introduced bishops and built diocesan cathedrals for them in the Romanesque style of England and France, their patronage of these sees increasing their claim to 'divine' authority. They also abandoned their old reliance on the more independent spiritual leadership of the monasteries.

But the kings never completely reassembled their English equivalents. They remained the representatives

The Seven Kingdoms

of their families and it is these dynasties that are remembered, rather than most of the individual rulers.

 ## The Kingdom of Tír Eoghain or Ulster

The O'Neills (Uí Néill) continued for several hundred years to dominate in the north, especially in Ulster, and they occasionally won the ceremonial high kingship. But, after Máel Sechnaill II, they never came close to extending that dominion into the rest of Ireland.

 ## The Kingdom of Thomond

The O'Briens, descendants of the family of Brian Boru, did not regain the high kingship but continued as overlords of North Munster with seats at Kincora, Killaloe, Dun na Scaith and Limerick and their capital, Cashel. The last great O'Brien king was Muirchertach (1093–1114). In the 12th century the dynasty suffered a serious defeat by the army of Connacht and after this the kingdom of Desmond rose to greater prominence in the south.

The Kingdom of Desmond

The MacCarthys were kings of the large territory of Desmond (South Munster), with their capital at Cork.

The Kingdom of Connacht

The O'Connor (Ua Conchobair) dynasty, expanding from its base in Roscommon, successfully displaced the O'Flahertys of Tuam and O'Kellys of Athlone to take control of Connacht. Important O'Connor kings included Turlough (d. 1156) and his son Ruaidhrí (d. 1198). Turlough was the most successful Irish warrior of the 12th century, a builder of forts and a navy, and he made a determined attempt to become master of Ireland, defeating Munster but dying before he could make the high kingship into an effective political power. The O'Connors continued to hold sway in the north-west of Ireland for many generations.

The Seven Kingdoms

The Kingdom of Breifne

Breifne was a kingdom centred round the upper Shannon, its rulers drawn from the O'Rourkes. With their capital at Cavan, they were hereditary enemies of the MacMurroughs of Leinster and had a long-standing quarrel over which of them should control the kingdom of Midhe, with its fertile agricultural land.

The Kingdom of Leinster

Ferns was the episcopal and royal capital of Leinster but an alliance with the Ostmen (or Vikings) who administered Dublin was often the basis of the power of these kings – the Uí Cheinnselaigh and then the MacMurroughs. The kings of Leinster were continually at war with their neighbours and it was through one of these disputes – the old quarrel with Breifne – that the ancient pattern of kingship in Ireland finally came to an effective end.

The Kingdom of Midhe (Meath)

This was an increasingly weak territory, though a fertile and desirable one. Its kingship was unstable and usually submitted to the kings either of Leinster or Breifne.

The End of Native Kingship in Ireland

The arrival of the Normans in 1169 was the first act in the long drama of British involvement with Ireland. It signalled the end of the High Kings and, ultimately, of all the indigenous Irish kingships. To make matters worse, the incomers were invited by an Irishman, Diarmit Mac Murchada, King of Leinster.

Diarmit, courageous and ambitious but not a far-sighted ruler, had in 1151 raided a neighbour, Tigernán Ua Ruairk, King of Breifne, and kidnapped his queen, Derbforgaill. Some writers on Irish history rank this episode with the abduction of Helen of Troy and it certainly had comparable consequences. The hostage was returned a year later, but Diarmit had now made an implacable enemy of Ua Ruairk, who was prepared to wait fifteen years for the death of Diarmit's protector, the High King Muirtertach Mac Lochlainn, before exacting revenge. Muirtertach had been succeeded at Tara by Ruadri Ua Conchobair of Connacht, son of Toirrdelbach (see above), and he agreed, with the help of some of Diarmit's discontented nobles and the Ostmen of Dublin, to attack Leinster. Diarmit was far outnumbered and fled to England.

He sought out Henry II and swore fealty to him. The English king, not averse to extending his power into Ireland, gave Diarmit leave to recruit military help among his Norman barons and Diarmit did so, with some success. He took a small but effective army back to Ireland, reducing the Ostman city of Wexford and forcing the *tuatha* of Leinster to submit. At this point even stouter support arrived from Wales, in the shape of the ambitious Norman Earl of Pembroke, who went by the name of Strongbow. Taking the field with this baron's well-armed knights and 1,500 Norman archers (against Irish who still used slingshot), Diarmit was poised to challenge for the high kingship itself. He and Strongbow had overwhelmed Waterford and then Dublin when, in 1171, Diarmit suddenly died at the age of sixty-one.

Strongbow, having sealed the pact with Diarmit by marrying his daughter Aifne, now expected to inherit the kingship of Leinster. A grand alliance of Celtic kings, led by the High King Ruaidri Ua Conchobair, tried to stop him, besieging the Normans in Dublin. But Strongbow broke out and quickly destroyed the much larger Irish army. Meanwhile, Henry II was becoming alarmed at Strongbow's success and decided on personal intervention. In a show of force, he arrived in Ireland with 400 ships and demanded that the Irish kings pay him homage. One by one they did so, no doubt with the same cheerful duplicity with which they habitually acknowledged their own High Kings.

Their action was seen rather differently in England, however. It was considered a permanent surrender of

The End of Native Kingship in Ireland

Ireland's sovereignty. Very gradually, from its base in the Pale (the narrow strip of land to the north and south of Dublin), the British crown enforced its claim to sovereignty over Ireland. Those of the subdued Irish dynasties that did not die out eventually dropped their royal titles and styled themselves, in the British way, as earls or barons. In this way, kingship in Ireland died away.

The last Irish ruler-chieftain to claim the high kingship itself was Brian O'Neill in 1258. The last dynastic uprising was as late as 1601, also by an O'Neill, Hugh, Earl of Tyrone. But by then it was impossible for him to call himself king at all.

FURTHER READING

Ashley, Mike, *British Monarchs* (London: Robinson, 1998).

Best, Nicholas, *The Kings and Queens of England* (London: Weidenfeld and Nicolson, 1995).

Best, Nicholas, *The Kings and Queens of Scotland* (London: Weidenfeld and Nicolson, 1999).

Brooke, Christopher, *The Saxon and Norman Kings* (London: Fontana, 1967).

Churchill, Winston S., *A History of the English Speaking Peoples*, Vols 1–3 (London: Cassell, 1956, 1957).

Fallow, Jeff, *Scotland for Beginners* (London: Writers and Readers, 1999).

Foster, Roy (ed.), *The Oxford History of Ireland* (Oxford: OUP, 1992).

Fraser, Antonia (ed.), *The Lives of the Kings and Queens of England* (London: Phoenix, 1997).

Harvey, John, *The Plantagenets* (London: Fontana, 1967).

Hibbert, Christopher, *The Story of England* (London: Phaidon, 1992).

Further Reading

Kearney, Hugh, *The British Isles* (Cambridge: CUP Canto, 1995).

Kenyon, J. P., *The Stuarts* (London: Fontana, 1966).

Linklater, Eric, *The Royal House of Scotland* (London: Sphere, 1972).

Lynch, Michael, *Scotland* (London: Pimlico, 1999).

Morris, Christopher, *The Tudors* (London: Fontana, 1966).

Plumb, J. H., *The First Four Georges* (London: Fontana, 1966).

Somerset Fry, Peter and Fiona, *History of Ireland* (London: Routledge, 1991).

Somerset Fry, Plantagenet, *The Kings and Queens of England and Scotland* (London: Dorling Kindersley, 1990).

Strong, Roy, *The Story of Britain* (London: Hutchinson, 1996).

Williamson, David, *The Kings and Queens of England* (London: National Portrait Gallery Publications, 1998).